COOKIEMANIA

COOKIEMANIA®

100 Irresistible Recipes
for Cookiemaniacs

JERI DRY AND ALIX ENGEL

CONTEMPORARY
BOOKS

CHICAGO · NEW YORK

Library of Congress Cataloging-in-Publication Data

Dry, Jeri.
   Cookiemania : 100 irresistible recipes for cookiemaniacs /
Jeri Dry and Alix Engel.
      p.   cm.
   Includes index.
   ISBN 0-8092-4551-5 (pbk.) : $7.95
   1. Cookies.   I. Engel, Alix.   II. Title.
TX772.D78   1988
641.8′654—dc 19   88-17517
                                             CIP

Cookiemania® is the registered trademark for Cookiemania, Inc.,
3231 West 37th Place, Chicago, IL 60632.

Published by Contemporary Books, Inc.
180 North Michigan Avenue, Chicago, Illinois 60601
Manufactured in the United States of America
Library of Congress Catalog Card Number: 88-17517
International Standard Book Number: 0-8092-4551-5

Published simultaneously in Canada by Beaverbooks, Ltd.
195 Allstate Parkway, Valleywood Business Park
Markham, Ontario L3R 4T8 Canada

This book is dedicated
to friendship

Contents

Acknowledgments

We wish to give special thanks to our mothers and grandmothers for their help and guidance, and for instilling within us the tradition of baking.

Preface

We think you, a fellow cookiemaniac, ought to know about Cookiemania's origins, and what propelled us, two close friends, mothers of teenagers, completely without any experience in the world of business, to start a company known the country over as bakers of "the world's finest cookies."

That isn't *our* quote! It comes from stacks of letters we receive constantly from recipients of our famous shiny red cookie tins.

Like all cookiemaniacs, cookies are in our blood: from the time we had to stand on footstools to reach the kitchen counters where our mothers were mixing doughs—and we, eager to assist, mostly licked the bowls—to the time six years ago when the avalanche of requests to "go into business" gave us the impetus to give it a try.

Both of us had extensive recipe collections, hand-me-downs from our mothers and grandmothers (and some that were handed down to them), and new recipes we created through years of trial and error.

We had always baked "for fun," and for the pleasure of giving gifts of cookies to our friends and teachers, making up Christmas, Easter, and various other holiday packages chock full of fresh, warm cookies.

Gathering courage from the urging of so many friends, we began to bake in quantity, still making every cookie by hand (as they are made today).

In the beginning, we baked in the tiny kitchens in our homes while the rest of the house served as packaging centers. Within a few months, the demand increased to the point where this was no longer feasible, and so we rented space on North Halsted Street in Chicago. But soon we grew to a staff of eight bakers, and the ever-increasing orders caused us to make another move to a large plant where today our handmade top-quality cookies are shipped to every corner of the globe.

And then we had a new request from our customers—publish a cookbook! So, we burned the midnight oil and culled our personal favorites from our vast files, presenting to you the best of Cookiemania. Some of these we do not make for sale because of limited shelf life, but we have baked and enjoyed each and every one and believe this book to be an outstanding compilation of very special cookie recipes.

Enjoy!

Jeri & Flix

Introduction

One of life's most savored moments is reaching into a cookie jar and discovering that someone has placed warm, fresh cookies in there just for you, her favorite cookiemaniac.

We've raised our children and founded our business on the premise that good, new, and original cookies are hard to come by. So we've kept our tins and canisters full of our favorites, which have kept our cookie-loving children, friends, and customers coming back in droves.

Words cannot describe the satisfaction and pleasure that can be derived from baking and serving cookies to your family and friends. Fun to make, baking cookies can be a terrific family project (that's how we got started and how our children became our official testers in later years). Fun to eat, friends can get together over cookies for tea or dessert, for a cookie decorating or creating party, or for a cookie swap, where you can trade recipes and hints, creating new sensations for your cookiemaniac.

Sweet or spicy, lemon or chocolate, nut or raisin, cookies occupy a special place in our hearts, and, we hope, in yours.

INGREDIENTS

Ingredients are the heart of any recipe, so here are some tips on what ingredients we use and why we use them.

1

Chocolate

There are so many different types of chocolate on the market these days that you must watch out for brands that are not consistent in taste, texture, and color. Also, beware of chocolates that are not completely pure, or that use artificial ingredients. We use only pure chocolate. The artificial "chocolate-flavored" chips are definitely cheaper, but you get what you pay for—a runny consistency, flat flavor, and sometimes a funny silky texture. There is a big difference in taste which we feel isn't compensated for by the lower price.

Florentines are the only cookie where we call for sweet chocolate (you can use a milk chocolate bar, if you like, either domestic or imported). All other cookies call for unsweetened or semisweet chocolate. Whether you use imported or domestic chocolate is a matter of personal taste. We use only Wilber Chocolate®, a quality domestic brand available in most specialty food shops.

Butter

In all of our recipes we use premium lightly salted butter, which we feel enhances the taste of the cookie. Butter will tell, we always tell our customers. If you should choose to substitute margarine, you should be aware that there is a slight difference in taste, and a greater difference in texture. But if you're watching your cholesterol intake, the difference is really nominal.

Salt

For those of you watching your sodium intake, unsalted butter can be substituted for the lightly salted variety with almost no difference in taste. All of the recipes can be made without salt, but the cookies will turn out a little flatter, though they will still taste delicious.

Bits 'o Brickle

We recommend you use Bits 'o Brickle® in some of our recipes because it is specifically designed for bakers who want to add chopped-up bits of peanut brittle to recipes. It is available in most grocery stores, and we feel it is the best product on the market for this purpose. But, in a pinch, any crushed-up plain (not covered with chocolate) peanut brittle will do nicely.

Extracts

We use only pure extracts—nothing artificial. Neilsen-Massey makes a fabulous vanilla extract, and it's the only one we use. Why? Well, when vanilla is the most important ingredient, as in our plain Butter cookie, using a mediocre vanilla will muddle the taste of the cookie.

Eggs

All the eggs called for in this book are extra large. If a recipe calls for egg yolks, freeze the whites for future use. Try freezing the individual whites in a small Pyrex custard cup. Once they have frozen, turn the cup over under hot running water until the white drops out. Transfer it to an individual plastic bag and return to the freezer. When you need one, leave it out at room temperature for an hour or so.

Nuts

Nuts are generally interchangeable or can be omitted at your discretion, except, of course, where nuts are the main ingredient. If the recipe calls for more than a half cup, do not omit the nuts, but you can replace them with an equivalent amount of dried fruit or cereal. Store unused nuts in a sealed container in the refrigerator or freezer for best keeping.

Lemon

Always try to squeeze your own lemon juice, but if you forget to buy lemons, Minute Maid® lemon juice in your supermarket freezer section is a nice alternative.

HELPFUL HINTS AND BAKING TIPS

We've discovered these hints through years of trial and error, baking hundreds of thousands of cookies for friends, family, and customers. We hope they help you make wonderful cookies.

Measuring Exactly

Accurate measuring is probably the single most important direction in the baking of delicious cookies. Even an eighth of a tablespoon too much salt or baking powder (for that matter, almost anything else) could prove disastrous in the oven. We use a straight-edged knife to level off a measuring spoon or cup. Don't use your finger or your "eye." Even Jeff Smith, the Frugal Gourmet, started off using a straight-edge. If you do choose to guestimate on amounts, please don't wonder if your cookies seem slightly off.

Oven Temperature

We recommend that you make sure your oven is calibrated correctly, which should weed out such problems as black-bottomed cookies. An easy, inexpensive way to check your oven's temperature is to freely hang a thermometer in your oven (one especially manufactured for that purpose) and test its true temperature.

And we can't stress enough the importance of preheating your oven. These recipes count on the dough hitting the oven at the precise temperatures indicated in each recipe. We recommend that the first thing you do is preheat your oven as directed.

The Difference Between Gas and Electric Ovens

As we mentioned above, it is very important to calibrate your oven so you know exactly how hot it gets. Logic still dictates that smaller ovens, whether gas or electric, will cook faster than larger ovens. A thermometer will help you regulate the heat accordingly. Electric ovens take much longer to cool down after baking is completed and heat up again after you open the door. Try to allow enough time to ensure the oven has fully reheated after each batch. We cook with gas, and have found that in gas ovens, the air circulates much more evenly.

For the Microwave Set

Although we say throughout the book to melt chocolate in the top of a double boiler, if you have a microwave oven then by all means use it. You'll save yourself some time. Simply use these directions for melting chocolate via the microwave instead of those for the stovetop method.

For two squares of chocolate: put the chocolate in a microwave ovenproof dish (we use a Pyrex custard cup) and cover with plastic wrap. Heat for 2 minutes at full power. Additional squares will need more time to melt, so check them every 30 seconds.

Greasing Pans

Many of the recipes do not require a greased pan, as we feel the cookie contains enough butter to self-grease. We recommend that you do not grease your pans unless the recipe specifically calls for it.

Cold Dough

When rolling refrigerator cookies, be sure the wax paper is straight, or it will leave a crease in your cookie.

INTO THE OVEN IT GOES

We bake only one cookie sheet at a time, which we place in the center of the oven. We've found that you get a much more uniform bake this way. There should be at least 2 inches of space between the cookie sheet and the sides of your oven so the air can circulate properly. Putting two sheets of cookies in the oven and rotating them will cool down your oven considerably and make a mess of your baking times. If you're in a hurry, we recommend you bake up a fresh batch of delicious bars.

All cookies should cool on a wire rack. Your cookie sheet will retain heat for quite a while and your cookies will continue to bake. Use an extra wide spatula to lift the entire cookie from the sheet onto the wire without breaking. Let bar cookies cool in their pan, cutting them into bars, squares, or triangles after they have cooled (don't let them get cold) unless otherwise specified.

And, make sure your cookie sheet has completely cooled before reusing. Cookies will start to spread and become misshapen if the sheets are still hot. Try to make all cookies on the same tray in the same shape, so they will bake evenly. Regrease after each use if greasing is necessary.

How to Cut Bars

If you're preparing a tray of bars, you don't want to cut them all the same size and shape. Try cutting some in a triangle, or a square, or a skinny finger-shaped rectangle, and this will make your party plate much prettier (also, if you cut the bars smaller, your guests will want to try them all!). For entertaining we like to cut a 1-inch square but for the purposes of this book, we have cut everything into a 2-inch square, which we consider to be a family-size cut, unless the recipe indicates otherwise.

Storing and Sending

In our homes, freshly baked cookies don't last very long—2 hours at most. But if your cookiemaniac is out, and you do get a chance to put some away, tins are wonderful. Not only do they make cute gift packages, but a good tin will last you a lifetime. Be sure to use a tight lid for soft cookies, and a looser lid for crisp varieties. Also, never mix crisp and soft together, or you'll end up with all the cookies going limp. And, you should avoid mixing such strong flavors as peppermint or peanut butter with other types of cookies, as you'll find the flavors mix together unpleasantly.

For long-term storage, use plastic containers wrapped in plastic wrap, then store in the freezer. Thaw the cookies in their containers for about 2 hours before you are ready to eat them.

If you plan on shipping your cookies to some lucky soul, do not use a box to mail fragile, thin, or very crisp cookies as you'll end up with crumbs! Instead, use your favorite tin, or even an empty, clean coffee can. Wrap two of the same type of cookie together in plastic wrap. The wrap will act as a cushion for each little cookie pack. Put two to three sheets of paper toweling between each layer, tape the lid on tightly, and pack into a cardboard carton using plenty of crumpled newspaper and stuffing for additional protection. And, be sure to mark the carton "Perishable—Fragile."

When you put so much of yourself into making these cookies, you want them to be received just the way you sent them—perfect and delicious!

A NOTE ON OUR HEARTS ♥

Eleven recipes are marked with a heart. The heart indicates one of the ten Cookiemania cookies we include in our tin of cookies we sell to the public. The extra one? This is a cookie we used to include (in our original tin) but don't anymore because of the perishability of this cookie and changing consumer demand.

1
It's All in the
Chocolate

Cake Brownies

Did you know there is a restaurant in Paris that makes hot chocolate from a chocolate bar? Don't miss un chocolat from Angelina, 226 Rue de Rivoli, Paris.

BROWNIE
½ cup butter
½ cup oil
1 cup water
4 tablespoons unsweetened
    cocoa
2 cups flour
2 cups sugar
2 eggs
1 teaspoon baking soda
½ cup buttermilk
1 teaspoon vanilla

FROSTING
½ cup butter
3 tablespoons unsweetened
    cocoa
⅓ cup buttermilk
1 box confectioners' sugar
1 cup chopped walnuts
1 teaspoon vanilla

1. Preheat oven to 350°F. Grease and flour a 9″ × 13″ baking pan. Mix butter, oil, water, and cocoa together in small saucepan and bring to a boil. Add this mixture to flour and sugar and beat until smooth.

2. Add eggs, baking soda, buttermilk, and vanilla. Mix well. Pour into prepared baking pan. Bake 20 minutes.

3. Prepare frosting while brownies are baking. Put all frosting ingredients in medium saucepan and heat. Do not boil.

4. Frost immediately after removing brownies from oven. Cut into squares when cool.

Makes 24 brownies

Caramel Brownies ♥

Chocolate lovers unite! From Ghirardelli Square to the Boston Tea Party, be on the lookout for events that celebrate a cookiemaniac's passion for chocolate.

1 14-ounce bag caramels
⅓ cup evaporated milk
2 4-ounce packages German
   sweet chocolate
6 tablespoons butter
4 eggs
1 cup sugar
1 cup flour, sifted
1 teaspoon baking powder
½ teaspoon salt
2 teaspoons vanilla
1 6-ounce package chocolate chips
1 cup chopped walnuts

1. Preheat oven to 350°F. Grease and flour a 9″ × 13″ baking pan. Combine caramels and evaporated milk in top of double boiler over low heat. Cover and simmer until caramels are melted, stirring occasionally. Set aside, keeping warm.

2. Combine German sweet chocolate and butter in 2-quart saucepan. Place over low heat, stirring occasionally until melted. Remove from heat. Cool to room temperature.

3. Beat eggs until foamy, using electric mixer at high speed. Gradually add sugar, beating until mixture is thick and lemon-colored.

4. Sift together flour, baking powder, and salt. Add to egg mixture, mixing well. Blend in cooled chocolate mixture and vanilla.

5. Spread half of mixture into prepared baking pan. Bake for 6 minutes. Remove from oven, and spread caramel mixture carefully over baked layer. Sprinkle with chocolate chips.

6. Stir ½ cup of the walnuts into the remaining chocolate batter. Spread batter by spoonfuls over the caramel layer. Sprinkle with remaining nuts.

7. Bake for 20 minutes. Cool in pan on rack. Refrigerate before cutting into bars or squares. These brownies are very difficult to cut if not chilled first.

Makes 25 brownies

Chocolate Banana Drops

Did you know there are more than 200 types of bananas in this world? Millions of bushels of the bright yellow variety we see most often in the States are consumed here each year.

2 squares (2 ounces) unsweetened chocolate
2½ cups flour, sifted
1½ teaspoons baking powder
½ teaspoon baking soda
½ teaspoon salt
⅔ cup butter
1 cup brown sugar, packed
2 eggs
1 teaspoon vanilla
1 cup mashed ripe bananas

1. Melt chocolate in top of double boiler over hot water.
2. Sift together flour, baking powder, baking soda, and salt. Set aside.
3. Cream butter. Add sugar and beat until fluffy. Add eggs, one at a time, beating well after each addition. Stir in vanilla and melted chocolate. Mix in flour mixture, alternating with bananas.
4. Cover and refrigerate at least one hour.
5. Preheat oven to 400°F. Drop dough by teaspoonfuls, 2 inches apart, onto ungreased cookie sheet. Bake about 12 minutes.
6. Remove from cookie sheet when warm and cool on rack. While cookies are cooling, prepare the frosting. (Use recipe following or see Index for Sour Cream Chocolate Drops frosting.)

Makes 60 cookies

Chocolate Fudge Frosting

1 6-ounce package semisweet chocolate chips
¼ cup butter
1 teaspoon vanilla
1½ cups confectioners' sugar, sifted
½ cup milk or half-and-half

1. Melt chocolate chips and butter together in medium saucepan over low heat. Stir often and cool slightly, continuing to stir.

2. Add vanilla and blend in sugar, alternating with milk or half-and-half. Beat well.

Makes enough frosting to cover 60 cookies

Chocolate Coconut Crispies

Chocolate comes in many forms, and since 1982 we've seen chocolate festivals, tastings, celebrations, even a chocolate cruise. Ahoy, mates.

2½ **cups flour, sifted**
½ **teaspoon baking soda**
½ **teaspoon salt**
2 **ounces unsweetened chocolate**
1 **cup butter**
2½ **cups brown sugar, firmly packed**
2 **eggs**
½ **cup walnuts, chopped**
½ **cup flaked coconut**

1. Preheat oven to 350°F. Grease a cookie sheet. Sift together already-sifted flour, baking soda, and salt. Set aside.

2. Melt chocolate in top of double boiler over hot water. Remove from heat and set aside.

3. Cream together butter and brown sugar. Add eggs and beat until light and fluffy. Add melted chocolate and beat well. Add flour mixture. Mix well. Stir in walnuts and coconut.

4. Drop by teaspoonfuls, 2 inches apart, onto prepared cookie sheet. Bake 12–15 minutes.

Makes 60 cookies

Chocolate Macaroon Bars

Everyone knows chocolate is a product made from the cocoa tree, which is native to tropical South America and cultivated in West Africa. But did you know that the seeds grow directly on the trunk?

COOKIE
4 ounces unsweetened chocolate
1 cup butter
2 cups sugar
1 cup flour
¼ teaspoon salt
1 teaspoon vanilla
3 eggs

FILLING
3 cups flaked coconut
1 (14-ounce) can sweetened
   condensed milk
½ teaspoon almond extract

TOPPING
1 6-ounce package semisweet
   chocolate chips
½ cup chopped walnuts

1. Preheat oven to 350°F. Grease a 9″ × 13″ baking pan. In a large pot melt unsweetened chocolate and butter over low heat. Remove from heat and set aside. Add sugar, flour, salt, vanilla, and eggs to chocolate mixture. Mix well. Spread one half of batter into prepared pan.

2. In mixing bowl, combine coconut, condensed milk, and almond extract. Mix well. Spoon filling over chocolate batter. Spread evenly to cover. Carefully spread balance of chocolate batter over filling.

3. Bake for 35–40 minutes, until edges are set. Remove from oven and sprinkle immediately with chocolate chips. Let stand one minute, spread evenly to cover. Sprinkle with chopped walnuts. Refrigerate. Cut into bars.

Makes 36 bars

Chocolate Marshmallow Bars

Did you ever have s'mores at camp as a kid? Well, this recipe grew out of a tradition of s'mores, campfires, kids, counselors, cookouts, insect repellent, and all the other wonderful memories of summers spent away from home.

2 ounces unsweetened chocolate
½ cup butter
1 cup sugar
2 eggs
½ cup flour
1 teaspoon vanilla
1 cup chopped pecans
16 large marshmallows

1. Preheat oven to 350°F. Grease an 11½″ × 7″ baking pan. Melt chocolate and butter in top of double boiler over hot water. Set aside.

2. Cream sugar and eggs until light and fluffy. Add flour. Beat. Add melted chocolate and butter. Beat well. Mix in vanilla and pecans.

3. Pour into prepared pan. Bake 18 minutes. Remove from oven and cover with marshmallows. Return to oven and bake until marshmallows are lightly browned.

4. Cool slightly and cut into bars.

Makes 16 bars

Chocolate Meringue Macaroons

A word of warning to the person who loves to give away cookies to fellow cookiemaniacs: these fancy party cookies are not hardy enough to withstand the U.S. mail service, and we're not sure they could even withstand overnight service. The meringue tends to either break apart or get soggy relatively quickly. We suggest you serve these within a few hours of making them.

COOKIE
½ cup butter, softened
½ cup granulated sugar
½ cup dark brown sugar, firmly packed
2 egg yolks
3 ounces unsweetened chocolate
1 teaspoon vanilla
1¾ cups flour
½ teaspoon baking powder
¼ teaspoon baking soda
¼ teaspoon salt
⅓ cup milk

MERINGUE TOPPING
2 egg whites
⅛ teaspoon salt
¼ cup sugar
1 cup flaked coconut
1 tablespoon flour

1. Preheat oven to 375°F. Grease two large cookie sheets. Cream butter, sugars, and egg yolks until fluffy, scraping sides of bowl.
2. Melt chocolate in top of double boiler over hot water. While chocolate is melting, add vanilla to butter mixture and then blend butter mixture with melted chocolate.
3. In separate bowl combine flour with baking powder, baking soda, and salt. Add to chocolate mixture alternating with milk. Beat until just blended and set aside.
4. Prepare topping. Beat egg whites and salt until stiff, gradually adding the sugar. Fold in coconut and flour, set aside.

5. Drop chocolate batter by rounded teaspoonfuls, 2 inches apart, onto prepared cookie sheets. Top each with ½ teaspoon meringue.

6. Bake for 6–8 minutes until lightly browned (cookies will be soft). Cool on wire rack.

Makes 54 cookies

Chocolate-Nut Refrigerator Cookies

The world's largest chocolate bar, a one-ton concotion, was the centerpiece of the sixth annual Great American Chocolate Festival, held (where else?) in Hershey, Pennsylvania. The giant bar contained more than 6 million calories!

¾ **cup butter**
½ **cup dark corn syrup**
2 **ounces unsweetened chocolate, melted**
⅔ **cup light brown sugar, packed**
1 **egg**
1 **teaspoon vanilla**
3 **cups flour**
¼ **teaspoon salt**
1 **cup chopped pecans**

1. Cream butter, syrup, melted chocolate, and sugar until light and fluffy. Beat in egg. Scrape bowl. Beat in vanilla. Scrape bowl. Sift flour and salt. Sift again and add to creamed mixture a little at a time. Beat until well blended. Stir in chopped nuts.

2. Shape into two logs 2 inches in diameter; wrap well in wax paper and refrigerate 8 hours or overnight.

3. Preheat oven to 350°F. Remove logs from refrigerator one at a time. Cut into ⅛-inch slices with a very sharp knife. Place onto cookie sheet 1 inch apart. Bake 10–12 minutes. Cool on wire rack.

Makes 70 cookies

Chocolate Mint Sticks

We're veterans of dozens of cookie swaps over the years (hosted our own or attended others). It's a fun way to spend a few hours with your friends and sample some delicious cookies as well. This is how it works: everyone brings extra copies of a favorite cookie recipe (plus enough samples for the crowd) and then swaps with everyone else. And that's how we got this recipe.

COOKIE
2 eggs
½ cup butter, melted
1 cup sugar
2 squares (2 ounces) unsweetened
    chocolate, melted
½ teaspoon peppermint extract
½ cup flour
½ cup ground almonds

PEPPERMINT FILLING
2 tablespoons butter
1 tablespoon heavy cream
1 cup confectioners' sugar, sifted
1 teaspoon peppermint extract

FROSTING
1 square (1 ounce) semisweet
    chocolate
1 tablespoon butter

1. Preheat oven to 350°F. Grease a 9″ square baking pan. Beat eggs. Add melted butter and sugar. Beat well. Add melted chocolate and peppermint. Beat. Add flour and nuts. Mix well. Pour ingredients into prepared pan and bake 25–30 minutes until cake tester or toothpick inserted in center comes out clean. Remove from oven and set on trivet or rack to cool.

2. Prepare filling. In small bowl, thoroughly blend butter and cream. Add sugar and peppermint. Mix well. Spread evenly over cooled baked layer.

3. Prepare frosting. Melt chocolate and butter together in small pan over low heat.

4. When filling is completely firm, spread frosting mixture on top.
5. Refrigerate until chocolate is firm. Cut into ¾- by 2¼-inch strips.

Makes 40 cookies

Chocolate Munchies

Rich, thick, and very chocolately, these cookies really pack a punch, and are sure to get you fired up with energy.

>   1 cup semisweet chocolate chips
>   8 marshmallows
>   1 tablespoon water
>   ¾ cup flour, sifted
>   ½ cup sugar
>   ¾ teaspoon salt
>   ½ teaspoon baking soda
>   ½ cup butter, softened
>   ⅓ cup brown sugar, firmly packed
>   1 egg
>   2 teaspoons almond extract
>   ½ teaspoon vanilla
>   1¼ cups oats, quick-cooking
>   1 cup chopped pecans

1. Preheat oven to 350°F. Grease a cookie sheet. Melt chocolate chips in top of double boiler over hot water. Add marshmallows and water; stir until melted and then remove from heat and set aside.

2. Sift together already-sifted flour, sugar, salt, and baking soda. Slowly blend butter, brown sugar, egg, almond extract, and vanilla into sifted ingredients. Mix well. Stir oats, pecans, and melted chocolate into batter; blend thoroughly.

3. Drop dough by teaspoonfuls, 2 inches apart, onto prepared cookie sheet. Bake 12–15 minutes.

4. Remove from cookie sheet immediately and cool on rack.

Makes 48 cookies

Chocolate Puffs

Light and airy, these Chocolate Puffs are sure to melt quickly on the tip of your tongue. The secret to making these cookies is to be certain the egg whites are extremely stiff. If your peaks bend at the top, keep whipping.

> 1 6-ounce package semisweet
>   chocolate chips
> 2 egg whites
> ½ cup sugar
> 1 teaspoon vanilla
> 1⅓ cups flaked coconut
> ½ cup chopped walnuts

1. Preheat oven to 300°F. Melt chocolate chips in top of double boiler over hot water and then set aside.

2. Beat egg whites until stiff. Gradually add sugar and continue beating until thoroughly blended. Stir in vanilla. Fold in melted chocolate, coconut, and walnuts.

3. Drop by teaspoonfuls, 1 inch apart, onto ungreased cookie sheet. Bake 10–15 minutes or until set.

Makes 36 cookies

Chocolate Shortbread Logs

Shortbread: quintessentially British, but without a doubt, the Scottish national cookie. Chocolate: quintessentially universal in appeal.

> **COOKIE**
> 1 cup butter
> 2 cups flour
> ½ cup confectioners' sugar, sifted
> 1 teaspoon vanilla
>
> **FROSTING**
> 1 6-ounce package semisweet chocolate chips
> 1 tablespoon butter
> ½ cup pecans or pistachio nuts, chopped fine

1. Preheat oven to 350°F. Cream butter. Add flour, confectioners' sugar, and vanilla. Blend well.

2. Using one teaspoonful of dough for each cookie, shape with hands into 2-inch long logs. Place 1 inch apart onto ungreased cookie sheet. Bake 13 minutes. Remove from cookie sheet while warm and cool thoroughly on wire rack.

3. Prepare frosting. Melt chocolate chips and butter in top of double boiler over hot water.

4. Dip one end (or both ends) of each cookie into chocolate and place on a cookie sheet lined with wax paper. Sprinkle nuts on chocolate. Refrigerate until firm (about 1 hour).

Makes 72 cookies

Chocolate Snowballs

Chocolate on the inside, white on the outside, this cookie should fool your favorite chocophile with its gooeyness. For variation, try substituting hazelnuts for the pecans.

> 1¼ cups butter
> ⅔ cup sugar
> 2 teaspoons vanilla
> 2 cups flour, sifted
> ⅛ teaspoon salt
> ½ cup unsweetened cocoa
> 2 cups finely chopped pecans
> Confectioners' sugar

1. Preheat oven to 350°F. Cream butter well; add sugar gradually and continue beating until light and fluffy. Stir in vanilla. Sift together flour, salt, and cocoa; add to butter mixture gradually, blending thoroughly. Add pecans and mix well.

2. Pinch off dough and using palms of hands, roll into balls the size of a marble. If dough is too soft to handle, chill for about 1 hour.

3. Place dough balls, 1 inch apart, onto ungreased cookie sheet. Bake for 18 minutes. Remove to wire rack to cool and then roll in confectioners' sugar.

Makes 70 cookies

Chocolate Sprinkles ♥

Another one from the original tin, these cookies taste just like a piece of flourless chocolate cake: soft, gooey, and chocolately on the inside.

¼ **cup unsalted butter**
6 **ounces semisweet chocolate**
2 **ounces unsweetened chocolate**
¾ **cup brown sugar, firmly packed**
2 **eggs**
⅛ **cup hot water**
2 **teaspoons vanilla**
¼ **cup flour**
¼ **teaspoon baking powder**
12 **ounces semisweet chocolate chips**
7 **ounces chopped walnuts**
Chocolate shots

1. Melt butter, 6 ounces semisweet chocolate, and 2 ounces unsweetened chocolate in top of large double boiler over hot water. When smooth, remove from hot water, and using hand electric mixer, blend in sugar, eggs, hot water, vanilla, flour, and baking powder. Mix well. Add chocolate chips and walnuts and stir by hand with wooden spoon.

2. Divide mixture in half and put in two bowls. Cover well and refrigerate at least 2 hours.

3. Fill small bowl with chocolate shots. Preheat oven to 300°F. Remove one bowl of dough at a time from refrigerator. Using two teaspoons, shape dough into ½-inch balls and drop into bowl of chocolate shots. Roll each ball in chocolate shots and place, 2 inches apart, onto ungreased cookie sheet.

4. Bake for 10 minutes. Cookies will be soft. Leave on cookie sheets to cool. They will "set" as they cool. Transfer to container or tray when completely cool.

Makes 150 cookies

Chocolate Swirl Bars

This is an old recipe we originally got from a neighbor, which we've refined a bit over the years. The principal ingredients are cream cheese and chocolate, which are marbleized by swirling the cheese and chocolate with the tip of a knife. Be careful not to swirl the mixture too much, or you will end up with light chocolate bars instead of Chocolate Swirl Bars.

CREAM CHEESE MIXTURE
2 3-ounce packages cream cheese, softened
2 eggs
¼ cup sugar
2 tablespoons flour
2 tablespoons butter, softened
½ teaspoon grated orange rind

CHOCOLATE MIXTURE
2 ounces unsweetened chocolate
¾ cup flour, sifted
½ teaspoon baking soda
¾ cup sugar
½ teaspoon salt
⅓ cup buttermilk
¼ cup butter, softened
1 egg
½ teaspoon vanilla

    1. Preheat oven to 350°F. Grease a 9″ square pan. Combine all ingredients for cream cheese mixture and beat until light and creamy. Pour into prepared pan.
    2. Prepare chocolate mixture. Melt chocolate in top of double boiler over hot water.
    3. Sift flour and baking soda together into mixing bowl. Add sugar and salt. Add buttermilk, butter, and melted chocolate. Beat well. Add egg and vanilla. Beat 2 minutes.
    4. Spoon chocolate mixture over cheese mixture in pan; run knife through, zigzagging several times to marbelize.
    5. Bake 40–45 minutes. Cool. Cut into squares.

Makes 40 bars

Chocolate Syrup Brownies

Did you know that theobroma, *Greek for "food of the gods," is also the name of the cocoa tree, grown worldwide on the equator? These are the gooeyist, fudgiest, stickiest brownies in the book, pure ambrosia for chocoholics.*

BROWNIE
½ cup butter
1 cup sugar
4 eggs
1 12-ounce can chocolate syrup
1 cup flour
1 cup chopped walnuts

FROSTING
1½ cups sugar
6 tablespoons milk
6 tablespoons butter
1 cup semisweet chocolate chips

1. Preheat oven to 350°F. Grease a 9″ × 13″ baking pan. Cream butter and sugar. Add eggs, mix well. Add chocolate syrup. Mix. Add flour and nuts and blend thoroughly. Pour into prepared pan and bake for 30 minutes.

2. Prepare frosting. Bring sugar, milk, and butter to a boil in small saucepan, stirring frequently. Cook 30 seconds. Add chocolate chips to mixture, mixing well until melted. Spread on top of cooled brownies. Cut into squares.

Makes 24 brownies

Chocolate Thumbprints

This is a fancy party cookie with a twist: a piece of crushed peppermint candy sits on top! These cookies are real winners at Christmastime, and our customers tell us Santa likes them very much.

COOKIE
2 ounces unsweetened chocolate
1 cup butter, softened
1 cup sugar
1 teaspoon vanilla
¼ teaspoon salt
1 egg
2½ cups flour
Thimble (for pressing hole for filling)

FILLING
¼ cup butter, softened
2 cups confectioners' sugar
1 to 2 tablespoons milk
½ teaspoon vanilla
2 to 3 drops red food coloring
½ cup crushed peppermint candy

1. Melt chocolate in top of double boiler over hot water and set aside to cool.

2. Combine butter and sugar. Beat until creamy. Add vanilla, salt, melted chocolate, and egg and mix well. Add flour and beat, scraping bowl, until well blended. Wrap dough in wax paper and refrigerate 1 hour.

3. Preheat oven to 375°F. Remove dough from refrigerator. Using palms of hands, shape dough into 1-inch balls and place, 2 inches apart, onto ungreased cookie sheet. With a thimble make a hole in the center of each cookie.

4. Bake 8–10 minutes or until edges are set. Remove from cookie sheet and cool on wire rack. If indentation has baked out, press again with thimble immediately after removal from oven.

5. Prepare filling. Cream butter and confectioners' sugar. Add milk, vanilla, and food coloring and mix well. Fill each cookie with about ½ teaspoon of filling. Sprinkle with peppermint candy and press down lightly.

Makes 72 cookies

Cocoa Nuggets

Did you know that high-quality chocolate takes at least three months to produce (and one minute to eat!)? Since technology hasn't discovered a way to grow chocolate bars and chips on trees, all cocoa beans must go through a process of fermentation, drying, selection, blending, roasting, flavoring, and manufacturing. The best-quality chocolate requires upward of four months to produce!

COOKIE
1¾ cups flour, sifted
½ cup unsweetened cocoa
⅛ teaspoon salt
1 cup butter, softened
⅔ cup sugar
½ teaspoon vanilla
1 cup chopped walnuts

TOPPING
3 tablespoons confectioners' sugar
3 tablespoons unsweetened cocoa

1. In bowl combine flour, ½ cup cocoa, and salt. Set aside. Cream butter and sugar. Beat until light and fluffy. Add flour mixture and vanilla and beat just until well blended. Stir in nuts. Wrap dough in wax paper and refrigerate at least 2 hours.

2. Preheat oven to 350°F. Remove dough from refrigerator. Using two teaspoons, shape dough into 1-inch balls and place, 1 inch apart, onto ungreased cookie sheet. Bake for 12 minutes. Let stand on cookie sheet for 2–3 minutes before removing to wire rack to cool.

3. Prepare topping. In small bowl combine cocoa and confectioners' sugar. When cookies are cool enough to handle, roll them in mixture.

Makes 48 cookies

Creamy Chocolate Chip Cookies

A nutritional breakdown of chocolate chip cookies at four per serving: 205 calories, .8mg iron, 40g vitamin A, .06mg thiamine, .06mg riboflavin, 2g protein, 12g fat, 3.5g saturated fats, 24g carbohydrates, 14mg calcium.

> **1 8-ounce package cream cheese**
> ½ **cup unsalted butter**
> ½ **cup lightly salted butter**
> ¾ **cup sugar**
> ¾ **cup dark brown sugar,**
>   **firmly packed**
> **1 egg**
> **1 teaspoon vanilla**
> 2½ **cups flour**
> **1 teaspoon baking powder**
> ½ **teaspoon salt**
> **1 12-ounce package semisweet**
>   **chocolate chips**
> **1 cup walnuts, chopped**

1. Preheat oven to 375°F. In large bowl, combine cream cheese, butters, and sugars. Mix until well blended. Add egg and vanilla and beat well. Gradually add flour, baking powder, and salt. Mix well. Stir in chocolate chips and walnuts.

2. Drop by teaspoonfuls, 1½ inches apart, onto ungreased cookie sheet. Bake 11 minutes or until tops and edges start to brown. Cool on wire rack.

Makes 96 cookies

Double Chocolate Chip Cookies

One of the largest candy companies offers a candy-of-the-month lifetime membership for about $2,000. We figure if you give this present to a 25-year-old chocoholic who lives to be 75, that's 600 pounds of chocolate, or one heck of a lot of calories. (These are the kinds of word problems we like.)

½ cup butter
2½ ounces unsweetened chocolate
1 cup sugar
1 teaspoon vanilla
2 eggs
2 cups flour, sifted
1 teaspoon baking powder
½ teaspoon baking soda
½ cup sour cream
1 6-ounce package semisweet
   chocolate chips

1. Preheat oven to 350°F. Grease a cookie sheet. Melt butter and chocolate together in large saucepan over low heat. Remove pan from heat and add sugar, vanilla, and eggs. Beat well. Sift together the already-sifted flour, baking powder, and baking soda. Stir the flour mixture, alternating with the sour cream, into the chocolate mixture in the saucepan. Beat well. Stir in chocolate chips.

2. Drop by teaspoonfuls, 2 inches apart, onto prepared cookie sheet. Bake 15 minutes. Cool on wire rack.

Makes 60 cookies

Easy Chocolate Coconut Drops

A cocodemer is a tree also known as the double coconut. The tree grows 98 feet tall and the female flower, which produces nuts up to 20 pounds, takes 10 years to ripen. Don't try to shake down this tree!

1 14-ounce can sweetened condensed milk
2 ounces unsweetened chocolate
3 cups flaked coconut
1 teaspoon vanilla

1. Preheat oven to 350°F. Grease a cookie sheet. Melt condensed milk and chocolate together in top of double boiler over hot water. Cook about 10 minutes, stirring often. Mixture should be thick. Remove from heat; stir in coconut and vanilla.

2. Drop by teaspoonfuls, about 1 inch apart, onto prepared cookie sheet.

3. Bake 10–12 minutes or until brown. Remove from cookie sheet and cool on rack.

Makes 30 cookies

Fudge Brownies

The Swiss, from whom we get fine watches as well as good airline service, are, not surprisingly, the largest consumers of chocolate in the world. Passion abounds, however, as Americans do eat nearly $5 billion worth of chocolate yearly (half of what the Swiss eat and in fifth place overall).

1 cup butter
4 ounces unsweetened chocolate
4 eggs
Pinch salt
2 cups sugar
1 cup sifted flour
1 teaspoon baking powder
1 teaspoon vanilla
1 cup chopped pecans

1. Preheat oven to 325°F. Grease a 9″ square baking pan. Melt butter and chocolate in small saucepan over low heat. Stir to blend and set aside to cool.

2. Beat eggs until light yellow; add salt, sugar, flour, and baking powder. Beat well. Blend in cooled chocolate, vanilla, and pecans. Blend thoroughly.

3. Pour into prepared pan and bake 35–45 minutes or until knife inserted in center comes out clean. Cool before cutting.

Makes 36 brownies

Mocha Cookies

Crillo cacao trees, the most highly prized variety, account for only 10 percent of the world's cocoa crop. Crillo beans are desired for their fragrant and nutty nuances, not found in the more common forastere bean.

½ **cup butter**
¾ **cup sugar**
¼ **cup brown sugar, firmly packed**
1 **egg**
1½ **cups flour**
2 **tablespoons instant coffee powder**
   (but not freeze-dried crystals)
1 **teaspoon baking powder**
½ **teaspoon salt**
½ **teaspoon cinnamon**
2 **teaspoons vanilla**
1 **cup finely chopped walnuts**
1 **12-ounce package semisweet chocolate chips**

1. Preheat oven to 350°F. Cream butter. Add both sugars and beat well. Add egg and mix well. Add flour, coffee, baking powder, salt, cinnamon, vanilla, and ½ cup walnuts. Mix well. Wrap dough in wax paper and chill thoroughly in refrigerator (at least two hours).

2. Remove dough from refrigerator. Using rounded teaspoonfuls of dough, shape into balls using palms of hands and place, 2 inches apart, onto ungreased cookie sheet. Bake for 12–15 minutes.

3. Remove cookie sheet from oven and working quickly place 3–4 chocolate chips in the center of each hot cookie. When chocolate has softened, spread over top and sprinkle with balance of walnuts. Remove cookies to wire rack and cool.

Makes 36 cookies

Sour Cream Chocolate Drops ♥

*When your guests tell you your cookies are fabulous, tell them that profes-
sional tasters judge chocolate by the following eight criteria: appearance
(should have a silky sheen), aroma (should have a strong scent), "break"
(should break cleanly), melting (should melt evenly on your tongue), texture
(should be creamy), flavor (should be rich and well balanced), finish (should
have a pleasant and mellow aftertaste), and sweetness (how sweet depends
on the type of chocolate used).*

COOKIE
2 cups flour, sifted
½ teaspoon baking soda
¼ teaspoon salt
2 squares (2 ounces)
    unsweetened chocolate
½ cup butter
1 cup brown sugar, packed
1 egg
1 teaspoon vanilla
¾ cup sour cream

FROSTING
1 6-ounce package semisweet chocolate chips
3 tablespoons butter
1 tablespoon hot water

1. Preheat oven to 350°F. Grease a cookie sheet. Sift together already-
sifted flour, baking soda, and salt and set aside.

2. Melt chocolate in small saucepan over low heat and set aside to cool.

3. Cream butter. Add brown sugar and beat. Add egg and vanilla and beat
until light and fluffy. Blend in cooled chocolate. Add sour cream, alternating
with dry ingredients (flour, salt, and baking soda). Begin and end with sour
cream. Beat and scrape bowl after each addition. Do not overbeat. Dough
should be fluffy.

4. Drop by teaspoonfuls, 2 inches apart, onto prepared cookie sheet. Bake
10 minutes.

5. Remove from cookie sheet when warm and cool on racks.

6. Prepare frosting. Melt chocolate chips with butter and hot water in small pan over low heat. Let cool and thicken so frosting will mound on cookie.

7. When cookies are completely cooled put a dollop of frosting on each one, using a knife or pastry bag.

Makes 60 cookies

Toffee Chip Squares♥

The longer we make these treats, the more popular they become. We didn't originally include them in our tin, but you can find them there now.

COOKIE
1 cup butter
¾ cup brown sugar
1 teaspoon vanilla
2¾ cups flour
½ teaspoon baking powder

TOPPING
1 6-ounce bag semisweet chocolate chips
3 tablespoons butter
1 tablespoon water
Bits 'o Brickle baking chips

1. Preheat oven to 350°F. Cream butter. Add brown sugar and vanilla. Mix well. Add flour and baking powder and mix until well blended.

2. Pat evenly into ungreased 9″ × 13″ baking pan. Press down flat. Bake 10–15 minutes until golden. Remove from oven and cut while warm into triangles, cut from 2″ squares.

3. Prepare topping. Melt chocolate chips, butter, and water in top of double boiler over hot water. Stir until smooth. Remove top of double boiler from hot water. Let chocolate thicken a little and then drop a large dollop in the center of each square or triangle.

4. Sprinkle Bits 'o Brickle chips on top of wet chocolate, heavily. Refrigerate to set. Remove squares with spatula and shake off excess Bits 'o Brickle.

Makes approximately 96 squares

Toffee-Filled Brownies

On average (but what is average to the average cookiemaniac?), more than 11 pounds of chocolate makes its way into the American stomach each year. Averages are nice, but we figure that adult chocoholics and kids account for approximately 97 percent of all chocolate eaten. Roughly, we estimate the average kid/chocoholic consumes close to 50 pounds per year. Now, that's an average we can relate to.

BROWNIE
1 cup flour
⅓ cup unsweetened cocoa
½ teaspoon baking powder
½ teaspoon salt
½ cup butter
1¼ cups sugar
3 eggs
1 teaspoon vanilla
1 cup finely chopped walnuts

FILLING
1 cup flaked coconut
1 egg
½ cup evaporated milk
¼ cup butter
1 cup brown sugar, firmly packed
1 tablespoon flour
⅛ teaspoon salt
1 teaspoon vanilla

1. Preheat oven to 350°F. Grease and flour a 9″ square baking pan. Sift together flour, cocoa, baking powder, and salt. Set aside.

2. Melt butter in small saucepan. Stir in sugar. Cool to lukewarm. Transfer to mixing bowl and blend in eggs, one at a time, beating well after each one. Add flour and cocoa mixture. Mix well. Stir in vanilla and walnuts. Spread into prepared pan.

3. Bake 30–35 minutes until brownie springs back when touched lightly in center. Cool 10 minutes. Invert onto rack and invert once again. Cool completely. Cut into 16 squares.

4. Prepare filling. Toast coconut by spreading on cookie sheet. Bake at 350°F for 10–12 minutes, stirring occasionally until golden brown. Set aside. Beat egg in a medium saucepan. Add milk, butter, brown sugar, flour, and salt. Bring to a boil over medium heat. Cook until thick, stirring constantly. Stir in vanilla and coconut. Cool.

5. Split each brownie in half and fill. Put back together, cover, and refrigerate.

Makes 16 brownies

White Chocolate Brownies

"White chocolate has much in common with Rodney Dangerfield—it has received little respect."
—Janice Wald Henderson,
White Chocolate

6 tablespoons unsalted butter
8 ounces white chocolate, grated
2 eggs
½ cup sugar
1 tablespoon vanilla
1 cup flour
1 heaping cup semisweet
   chocolate chunks

1. Preheat oven to 350°F. Grease and flour an 8″ square baking pan. Melt butter and 4 ounces of white chocolate together in top of double boiler over hot water. When melted, remove from heat and add balance of white chocolate. Stir to blend well. Set aside.

2. Beat eggs. Add sugar. Beat 2–3 minutes. Add white chocolate and butter mixture, vanilla, and flour. Beat just until smooth. Add chocolate chunks and mix in by hand—do not beat.

3. Pour into prepared pan and bake 35 minutes or until cake tester or tooth pick inserted in center comes out clean. Cool on trivet or wire rack. Cut into squares or bars.

Makes 24 brownies

Rocky Road Caramel Bars

The World Almanac *claims that six pounds of peanuts per person (try saying that one fast) were consumed in 1985.*

CRUST AND TOPPING
1 cup flour
¾ cup quick-cooking oats
½ cup sugar
½ cup unsalted butter, softened
½ teaspoon baking soda
¼ teaspoon salt
¼ cup salted peanuts, chopped

FILLING
½ cup caramel ice cream topping
½ cup salted peanuts, chopped
1½ cups miniature marshmallows
½ cup semisweet chocolate chips

1. Preheat oven to 350°F. Grease and flour a 9″ square baking pan. Combine flour, oats, sugar, butter, baking soda, and salt. With electric hand mixer, beat at low speed, scraping bowl often. Mixture should be crumbly. Stir in peanuts. Remove ¾ cup of mixture and set aside. Press balance of mixture into prepared pan. Bake in center of oven for 12–17 minutes or until lightly browned.

2. Remove from oven. Spread caramel topping evenly over hot crust. Sprinkle with peanuts, marshmallows, and chocolate chips. Crumble reserved topping mixture over chocolate chips. Return to oven and bake 20–25 minutes more or until topping mixture is lightly browned.

3. Remove from oven and let cool. Cover and refrigerate 2–3 hours or until firm. Cut into bars. Cover and keep in refrigerator.

Makes 30 bars

2
Fresh from the
Fruit Tree

Apple Raisin Cookies

Legend has it that walnuts are the nuts of kings. Well, king or pauper, walnuts add a heartiness to these cookies you'll enjoy biting into. Remember to use a Granny Smith apple, which will generally hold up better under baking.

½ cup butter
1 cup brown sugar, firmly packed
2 eggs
½ teaspoon vanilla
½ cup chopped walnuts
½ cup raisins
1 medium apple (preferably
    Granny Smith), chopped
    (seeds removed)
1¾ cups flour
½ teaspoon baking soda
½ teaspoon baking powder
1 teaspoon cinnamon
½ cup quick-cooking oats

1. Preheat oven to 425°F. Grease a cookie sheet. Cream butter. Add brown sugar. Beat well. Add eggs and vanilla and beat until light and fluffy. Add walnuts, raisins, and apple. Mix well. Stir in flour, baking soda, baking powder, cinnamon, and oats. Mix well.

2. Drop by teaspoonfuls, 1½ inches apart, onto prepared cookie sheet. Bake 10–12 minutes. Remove to wire rack to cool.

Makes 48 cookies

Applesauce Nut Cookies

Have you ever tried to make your own applesauce? It's so simple, you'll be making homemade applesauce every time you get a few apples together. Here's how: Cut up as many apples as you want into a pot, and cover with water. Boil until the apples are soft, then drain. Put the whole pieces into an apple masher (which will strain the sauce from the stem, seeds, and skin). Stir the sauce and sprinkle with cinnamon.

½ cup butter
½ cup brown sugar, firmly packed
½ cup sugar
1 egg
2 cups flour, sifted
½ teaspoon cinnamon
¼ teaspoon salt
¼ teaspoon baking soda
1 teaspoon baking powder
½ cup applesauce
¼ cup raisins
½ cup chopped walnuts
1 teaspoon vanilla

1. Preheat oven to 400°F. Cream butter and sugars. Add egg and mix until light and fluffy. Sift together already-sifted flour, cinnamon, salt, baking soda, and baking powder; add to creamed mixture and blend well. Add applesauce, raisins, walnuts, and vanilla. Mix well.

2. Drop by teaspoonfuls, 1½ inches apart, onto ungreased cookie sheet. Bake 10 minutes or until brown. Remove to wire rack to cool.

Makes 30 cookies

Apricot Bars

The nice thing about dried apricots is this: the longer they sit, the better they get. Although you'll only need ⅔ cup for this recipe, get a few extra. If you're like us, you won't be able to wait until these babies are out of the oven.

CRUST
1 cup flour, sifted
¼ cup sugar
½ cup butter, softened

TOPPING
⅔ cup dried apricots
⅓ cup flour
½ teaspoon baking powder
¼ teaspoon salt
2 eggs
1 cup brown sugar, packed
½ teaspoon vanilla
Confectioners' sugar

1. Rinse apricots. Put in medium saucepan and cover with water. Boil ten minutes. Drain well, cool, and chop coarsely. Set aside.

2. Preheat oven to 350°F. Grease an 8″ square baking pan. Mix 1 cup flour and sugar together in bowl. Cut in butter until crumbly. Pat into prepared pan. Bake 25 minutes.

3. Prepare topping. Sift together ⅓ cup flour, baking powder, and salt and set aside. Beat eggs. Add brown sugar and blend well. Mix in flour mixture, vanilla, and apricots. Spread over baked crust.

4. Return to oven for 30 minutes. Cool on trivet or rack. Cut into squares. Sprinkle with confectioners' sugar.

Makes 32 bars

Apricot Chews

We're pretty sure Kellogg's got the idea for their Fruit Chews® cereal from us. Our Apricot Chews make a wonderful, chewy, fruity "breakfast cereal" bar, which, with milk, juice, and coffee, should get your day started right.

½ cup finely chopped dried apricots
½ cup golden raisins
⅓ cup water
1 cup flour, sifted
1 teaspoon baking powder
¼ teaspoon baking soda
½ cup chopped walnuts
½ cup crushed pineapple, drained
2 eggs
1 tablespoon lemon juice
1 cup confectioners' sugar

1. Preheat oven to 350°F. Grease a 9″ square baking pan. Cook apricots and raisins in water 8–10 minutes or until tender. Drain well.

2. Combine flour with baking powder and baking soda. Add walnuts, pineapple, and drained apricots and raisins. Stir to mix well.

3. In small mixing bowl, beat eggs with lemon juice, just until foamy. Gradually add sugar, beating just until blended. Fold in flour and fruit mixture. Spread in prepared pan.

4. Bake 35–40 minutes until golden brown. Cut into bars while warm. Cover with confectioners' sugar.

Makes 24 bars

Apricot Oat Squares

Apricot Oat Squares are a quick and easy treat for you to whip up anytime. Try substituting other types of fruit preserves, such as strawberry, cherry, or raspberry, for variation in taste and color.

2 cups quick-cooking oats
1¾ cups flour
1 cup butter, softened
¾ cup brown sugar, firmly packed
1½ teaspoons cinnamon
½ teaspoon baking soda
1 cup apricot preserves

1. Preheat oven to 400°F. Grease a 9″ × 13″ baking pan. Mix together oats, flour, butter, sugar, cinnamon, and baking soda until crumbly. Remove 2 cups and set aside. Press remainder of oat mixture into bottom of prepared pan. Spread apricot preserves evenly on top. Crumble reserved oat mixture over preserves.

2. Bake 20 minutes or until golden brown. Cool, then cut into squares.

Makes 30 squares

Banana Chocolate Bars

A great-looking, great-tasting combination, guaranteed to perk up even the fifth day of Thanksgiving leftovers.

⅔ cup butter
⅔ cup dark brown sugar,
    firmly packed
⅔ cup sugar
1 egg
1 teaspoon vanilla
1 cup mashed ripe bananas
2 cups flour, sifted
2 teaspoons baking powder
½ teaspoon salt
1 6-ounce package semisweet chocolate chips

1. Preheat oven to 350°F. Grease a 10″ × 15″ × 1″ jelly roll pan. Cream butter with sugars until light and fluffy. Add egg and vanilla; beat well. Blend in bananas.

2. Sift together already-sifted flour with baking powder and salt; add to banana mixture gradually. Beat until smooth. Stir in chocolate chips.

3. Smooth into prepared pan. Bake 30 minutes. Remove from oven and cool completely before cutting.

Makes 48 bars

Coconut Apple Cookies

Coconut reminds us of hot summer days, long stretches of beach, clear tur-quoise water, and breezy nights. When you're in the Caribbean mood, a quick batch of these cookies might just get your palm tree swaying.

1 cup flour
½ teaspoon baking powder
½ teaspoon salt
½ teaspoon baking soda
½ cup butter
½ cup sugar
½ cup brown sugar, firmly packed
1 egg
2 teaspoons vanilla
½ cup quick-cooking oats
1 cup chopped peeled apple
2 cups flaked coconut

1. Preheat oven to 375°F. Mix flour with baking powder, salt, and baking soda. Set aside. Cream butter. Gradually add sugars and beat until light and fluffy. Blend in egg and vanilla. Add flour mixture. Beat, scraping bowl. Add oats, apple, and 1⅓ cups coconut.

2. Drop by teaspoonfuls, 1½ inches apart, onto ungreased cookie sheet. Sprinkle with remaining coconut.

3. Bake 10 minutes or until golden brown. Cool on wire rack.

Makes 48 cookies

Coconut-Chocolate Thumbprints

A cookie fact: cookie consumption (thanks in part to cookiemaniacs nation-wide) is on the rise. Industry research shows a 43 percent increase in the number of cookies eaten in 1987.

COOKIE
1 cup butter, softened
1 cup confectioners' sugar
½ teaspoon salt
2 teaspoons vanilla
2 cups flour
Thimble (for making hole for filling)

FILLING
1 cup confectioners' sugar
2 tablespoons flour
1 teaspoon vanilla
1 3-ounce package cream cheese, softened
½ cup coconut

FROSTING
½ cup semisweet chocolate chips
2 tablespoons water
2 tablespoons butter
½ cup confectioners' sugar

1. Preheat oven to 350°F. Prepare cookie dough. Cream butter, sugar, salt, and vanilla until light and fluffy. Blend in flour and mix well. Using a teaspoon-ful of dough, shape into ball with palms of hands. Place 2 inches apart onto ungreased cookie sheet. With thumb or large thimble make an indentation in center of each cookie.

2. Bake 12–16 minutes until lightly browned on edges. Remove from cookie sheet right away and cool on wire rack.

3. Prepare filling. In small bowl, cream sugar, flour, vanilla, and cream cheese until light and fluffy. Stir in coconut. Fill each cookie with about ½ teaspoon of filling.

4. Prepare frosting. In small saucepan, over low heat, melt chocolate chips with water and butter, stirring constantly. Remove from heat. Add sugar, blend until smooth. Drizzle over filling in cookies.

Makes 60 cookies

Coconut Squares

Packed with coconut, pecans, and brown sugar, these squares are three-dimensional bites bursting with the flavor of the cocodemer *tree.*

CRUST
½ cup butter, softened
1 cup flour
¼ cup brown sugar, firmly packed

FILLING
2 eggs
1½ cups brown sugar, firmly packed
3 tablespoons flour
½ teaspoon baking powder
1 teaspoon vanilla
¾ cup chopped pecans
1 cup flaked coconut

1. Preheat oven to 350°F. Grease an 8″ square baking pan. Mix together butter, flour, and brown sugar until crumbly. Press into bottom and 1 inch up sides of the prepared pan. Bake for 8 minutes. Remove from oven and set aside.
2. Prepare filling. Beat eggs together with brown sugar, flour, baking powder, vanilla, and pecans. Mix well. Pour over baked crust. Sprinkle with coconut. Return to oven and bake 40 minutes. Cool on rack. Cut into squares when cool.

Makes 16 squares

Coconut Apricot Balls

This recipe calls for the Thimble Twist, once a popular turn-of-the-century dance for matronly bakers. Legend has it that on cold, wintry Friday nights, all the matrons and their mates would gather around for the Twist, after which they'd feast on cookies, cakes, and cider.

> **1 cup butter**
> **⅔ cup sugar**
> **2 eggs, separated**
> **1 teaspoon vanilla**
> **2 cups flour**
> **1 teaspoon salt**
> **1 14-ounce bag flaked coconut**
> **Thimble (for making hole for filling)**
> **Apricot preserves***

1. Preheat oven to 300°F. Grease a cookie sheet. Cream butter and sugar. Add egg yolks and vanilla and beat well. Gradually blend in flour and salt and mix well.

2. In small bowl, lightly beat egg whites. Fill another small bowl with coconut.

3. Pinch off about 1 inch of dough and roll into ball using palms of hands. Dip ball into egg whites and then roll in coconut. Place 2 inches apart onto prepared cookie sheet.

4. When cookie sheet is filled, make an indentation in center of each ball with a thimble, twisting the thimble to widen hole. Twist thimble about ¾ of the way down into the ball of dough.

5. Bake 24 minutes. Remove from baking sheet while warm and fill with apricot preserves.

Makes 36 cookies

---

*Preserves are easier to work with if you put some in a small bowl and beat a few minutes until smooth. Use a small baby spoon or pastry bag to fill cookies.

Cranberry Oatmeal Cookies

We could have easily renamed these cookies "The Everything-Rolled-Up-Into-One Cookie," except that there's no chocolate! We find the buttermilk gives this cookie a special holiday taste.

1 cup butter, softened
¾ cup sugar
¾ cup brown sugar, firmly packed
½ cup buttermilk
2 eggs
2 cups flour
1 teaspoon baking powder
1 teaspoon baking soda
1 teaspoon cinnamon
½ teaspoon nutmeg
2 teaspoons grated orange peel
3 cups quick-cooking oats
1½ cups chopped cranberries
1 cup chopped walnuts

1. Preheat oven to 375°F. Grease a cookie sheet. Cream butter. Add sugars and beat until light and fluffy. Add buttermilk and eggs; beat well. Add flour, baking powder, baking soda, cinnamon, nutmeg, and orange peel; blend well. Add oats and mix well. Stir in cranberries and walnuts.

2. Drop by teaspoonfuls, 2 inches apart, onto prepared cookie sheet.

3. Bake 8–10 minutes or until golden brown around edges. Let sit on sheet for 1 minute, after baking, and then transfer to rack to cool.

Makes 80 cookies

Cranberry Orange Cookies

We've discovered that certain colors are associated with particular holiday seasons: orange leads the pack for fall and red surfaces for Christmas, Hannukkah, and New Year's. With these colors in mind, enjoy these "color-coordinated" cookies all fall and winter long.

COOKIE
¾ cup sugar
½ cup brown sugar, firmly packed
½ cup butter, softened
½ cup sour cream
1 teaspoon vanilla
2 eggs
2¼ cups flour
½ teaspoon baking soda
½ teaspoon baking powder
1½ cups chopped cranberries
½ cup chopped pecans

FROSTING
2 cups confectioners' sugar
2 tablespoons butter, melted
1 teaspoon grated orange rind
2-3 tablespoons orange juice

1. Preheat oven to 350°F. Lightly grease a cookie sheet. Combine sugars and butter and beat well. Add sour cream, vanilla, and eggs. Blend well. Add flour, baking soda, and baking powder and mix well. Stir in cranberries and nuts by hand. Do not overmix, or the cranberries will break up and become soupy.

2. Drop by teaspoonfuls, 2 inches apart, onto prepared cookie sheet. Bake 11-13 minutes or until golden brown. Remove at once from cookie sheet and cool on wire rack.

3. In small bowl combine all frosting ingredients and beat well. Spread over top of cooled cookies.

Makes 60 cookies

Jellies ♥

Jellies are one of our all-time favorite cookies. We adapted this old-fashioned thumbprint recipe to add color to our party and holiday plates. It fit the bill for us, and we hope you enjoy them as much as we do.

2 cups sifted flour
¼ teaspoon salt
1 cup butter
½ cup brown sugar, packed
2 egg yolks
½ teaspoon vanilla
1 cup pecans, chopped fine
Seedless raspberry preserves
Thimble (for pressing hole into cookie for filling)

1. Preheat oven to 350°F. Sift together already-sifted flour and salt and set aside. Cream butter and brown sugar together in mixing bowl. Add egg yolks and vanilla and beat until light and fluffy. Add flour and salt mixture, mix well.

2. Put pecans in small bowl. Pinch off enough dough to make a 1-inch ball using palms of hands to shape. Roll each ball gently in pecans and place 2 inches apart onto ungreased cookie sheet.

3. Bake for 5 minutes. Remove sheet from oven and make an indentation in the center of each ball, using a metal thimble or thumb. Press down about ¾ of the way into each ball.

4. Return tray to oven and bake an additional 8 minutes. Remove cookies from sheet and cool on wire rack.

5. When cookies are completely cool, fill indentation with preserves.

Makes 36 cookies

Frosted Raisin Cookies

Old baking folklore has it that frosting was originally invented to cover up a master baker's mistakes. It seems one of his cookies got a bit too brown on top (not to mention what the bottom looked like), so he whipped together a thick, sweet glaze to hide his error (he was probably a king's baker and was afraid of losing more than his baker's apron).

COOKIE
1¾ sticks unsalted butter,
    softened
¾ cup sugar
2 eggs
2¾ cups flour
1½ cups raisins

FROSTING
½ cup apricot jam
½ cup water
¼ cup confectioners' sugar

1. Preheat oven to 375°F. Grease a cookie sheet. Using an electric mixer, cream butter. Gradually add sugar and beat until light and fluffy. Beat in eggs. Stir in flour and raisins with wooden spoon.

2. Drop by rounded tablespoonfuls, 1 inch apart, onto prepared cookie sheet. Bake 12–15 minutes or until golden. Remove from cookie sheet and cool on rack.

3. Prepare frosting. Heat apricot jam with water over low heat, stirring until jam is melted. Remove from heat and stir in confectioners' sugar. Mix well. Frost cooled cookies.

Makes 32 cookies

Lemon Bars ♥

This is another cookie from the Cookiemania original tin. We're known for our lemon bars, and if you follow this recipe to the letter, you're sure to create a wonderful dessert. Many people have tried to imitate our bars, but have fallen way short. Funny enough, they come to us in a panic, buy enough bars for their party, and then pass them off as their own. Here, for the first time ever, is our recipe.

CRUST
2 cups flour
½ cup confectioners' sugar
Pinch of salt
1 cup butter, slightly softened

LEMON FILLING
2 cups sugar
4 tablespoons flour
Juice of 2 lemons (at least ⅓ cup)
Rind of 1 lemon
4 eggs
Confectioners' sugar (for topping)

1. Preheat oven to 350°F. Mix together flour, confectioners' sugar, and salt. Cut in butter or use food processor with quick on/off movements. Dough should be the consistency of meal—not smooth. Pat down well into ungreased 9″ × 13″ baking pan. Bake 20 minutes, until crust is golden. Remove from oven.

2. Prepare filling. Mix together all ingredients except confectioners' sugar and beat very well. Pour over baked crust. Filling should be poured over crust just after beating, do not let it sit while crust is baking. Return to oven and bake 20 minutes.

3. Cool completely on trivet or rack. Sprinkle heavily with powdered sugar and cut into squares.

Makes 48 bars

Orange Crisps

For years we've been told that orange juice wasn't just for breakfast anymore. We've taken orange juice off the table and used it to enhance the flavoring of these cookies. Why not try a cup of mandarin orange tea as you munch on the fruits of your labor?

2½ cups sifted flour
¼ teaspoon baking soda
¼ teaspoon salt
1 cup butter
½ cup sugar
½ cup brown sugar
1 tablespoon orange juice
1 teaspoon grated orange rind
1 egg

1. Preheat oven to 375°F. Sift together already-sifted flour with baking soda and salt and set aside.

2. Cream butter and sugars together; mix well. Add orange juice, orange rind, and egg and beat well. Gradually blend in flour mixture.

3. Roll dough out on floured board and use cookie cutters or fill cookie press and form on ungreased cookie sheet. Bake 10–12 minutes.

4. Remove from cookie sheets right away and put on wire rack to cool.

Makes 72 cookies

Peachy Spice Squares

When you finally try this recipe, you'll probably love it as much as we do. A version of this recipe originated with an old friend of Jeri's grandmother. This woman always told us these squares were delicious, but skeptics that we are, we were loath to use canned peaches. Silly us.

1½ cups flour
1 teaspoon cinnamon
½ teaspoon ginger
½ teaspoon allspice
½ teaspoon baking soda
1 teaspoon orange rind
½ cup butter
1 cup brown sugar,
    firmly packed
1 egg
1 16-ounce can cling
    peach slices, drained
1 cup raisins
½ cup chopped walnuts

1. Preheat oven to 350°F. Grease an 11″ × 16″ baking pan. Sift together flour, cinnamon, ginger, allspice, and baking soda. Add orange rind and set aside.

2. In large bowl, cream butter and brown sugar until light and fluffy. Beat in egg and well-drained peaches. Stir in flour mixture and mix well. Add raisins and walnuts. Blend well.

3. Spread evenly in prepared pan. Bake 15–20 minutes or until dough begins to pull away from sides of pan. Cool, then cut into squares.

Makes 30 squares

Raisin Bars

Sunny California is home to more than 7 zillion raisins annually. Some of these raisins go into packages with a sun on them, others go into bags, cartons, and other containers. Whichever raisins you choose, black or yellow, you'll love them in these bars.

CRUST
1 cup raisins
1 cup water
1 cup butter
1½ cups sugar
2 eggs
3 cups flour
1¼ teaspoons baking soda
½ teaspoon salt
½ teaspoon cinnamon

TOPPING
1 teaspoon cinnamon
2 tablespoons sugar

1. Preheat oven to 350°F. Grease a 12″ × 18″ × 1″ baking pan. Boil raisins in 1 cup of water. Drain well and set aside to cool.

2. Cream butter. Add sugar and eggs and beat until light and fluffy. Add flour, baking soda, salt, and cinnamon and mix well. Stir in cooled raisins.

3. Spread into prepared pan. Bake 15–20 minutes, until golden.

4. Prepare topping. Mix cinnamon and sugar together and sprinkle on top as soon as sheet is removed from oven. Cool and cut into strips or bars.

Makes 27 bars

Raspberry Meringues

Raspberries: those little plump red balls of sweetness that really pop out at you in this recipe. We suggest you serve them with lemon sorbet and fresh raspberries for a light, delicious dessert.

3 egg whites, at room temperature
¼ teaspoon cream of tartar
Dash of salt
¾ cup sugar
¼ cup raspberry preserves, seedless
5-6 drops red food coloring

1. Preheat oven to 225°F. Cover cookie sheet with aluminum foil. In small bowl, with electric hand mixer, beat egg whites, cream of tartar, and salt until soft peaks form. Gradually add sugar, beating until very stiff peaks form, about 10 minutes. Add preserves and food coloring and beat one minute at highest speed of mixer.

2. Drop by teaspoonfuls, 2 inches apart, onto foil-lined cookie sheet. Bake for 2 hours. Cool completely. Peel off of foil.

Makes 36 cookies

Raspberry Oatmeal Bars

We've suggested frozen raspberries but if you have fresh, by all means use them. This recipe adapts well to all sorts of berries, so feel free to try blueberries and strawberries.

CRUST
1½ cups flour
1 cup brown sugar, firmly packed
1 cup quick-cooking oats
½ teaspoon cinnamon
1 teaspoon vanilla
½ cup butter, melted

FILLING
2 10-ounce packages frozen
    raspberries
1½ tablespoons cornstarch
2 tablespoons cold water
½ cup sugar

1. Preheat oven to 325°F. Combine flour, brown sugar, oats, and cinnamon. Mix together. Add vanilla and melted butter and blend until crumbly. Remove 2 cups of mixture and press into a 9″ square ungreased baking pan. Set aside.

2. Prepare filling. Drain raspberries, reserving juice. Add enough water to the juice to make 1 cup. Put into saucepan. Dissolve cornstarch in 2 tablespoons cold water and add to raspberry juice with sugar. Cook over medium heat, stirring until thick and clear. Remove from heat and add drained raspberries. Spread over crust. Sprinkle with remaining oatmeal crumbs.

3. Bake for 55–60 minutes or until top is browned. Remove from oven and cool before cutting into squares.

Makes 16 bars

3
It's Nuts to Us

Almond Bars

We all know almonds have been a joy for centuries; it's just tough to crack the shells without shattering the meat inside. Preshelled almonds are a good, timesaving substitute to cracking your own.

CRUST
1¼ cups flour
¼ cup sugar
½ cup butter

FILLING
3 tablespoons butter, softened
½ cup sugar
1 egg
½ cup almonds, ground
1 tablespoon flour
½ teaspoon almond extract

TOPPING
3 tablespoons butter
¼ cup sugar
½ cup sliced almonds
1 tablespoon flour
2 teaspoons milk
½ teaspoon almond extract

1. Preheat oven to 350°F. Combine flour and sugar. Cut in butter until mixture resembles cornmeal. Pat into bottom of a 9″ × 13″ × 2″ baking pan and set aside.

2. Prepare filling. Cream butter and sugar until fluffy. Beat in egg. Stir in almonds, flour, and almond extract. Mix well. Spread evenly over crust*. Bake for 25 minutes or until filling is golden brown and firm to the touch. Remove from oven and cover with topping.

3. Combine all topping ingredients in small saucepan over low heat. Stir and heat thoroughly. Spread evenly over already-baked crust and filling. Broil 6 inches from heat until topping is golden, about 3 minutes. Cool on rack. Cut into bars.

Makes 48 bars

---

*This mixture can be difficult to spread. However, after 1 minute in the oven it will spread evenly.

Hazelnut Bites

Hazelnuts, or filberts, come from a tree whose name we can't pronounce. Though they're grown all over the world, European hazelnuts are considered the superior variety. We buy American.

Until 1940, most hazelnuts were imported from Italy. Since then, when orchards were planted all over the Pacific Northwest, the West Coast has consistently produced one of the largest crops in the world. No wonder people say California has the most "nuts."

COOKIE
1½ cups flour
½ cup sugar
½ cup butter, softened
1 egg
1 tablespoon vanilla
1 5-ounce can hazelnuts*

FROSTING
¼ cup semisweet chocolate chips
1 teaspoon butter

1. Preheat oven to 350°F. Knead together flour, sugar, butter, egg, and vanilla by hand. Dough will be stiff. Using a teaspoonful of dough, shape around a hazelnut; roll into a ball.

2. Place 1 inch apart onto ungreased cookie sheet. Bake 8–10 minutes. Remove from cookie sheet and cool on wire rack.

3. Prepare frosting. Melt chocolate chips and butter together in a small saucepan over low heat. Drizzle over cooled cookies.

Makes 60 cookies

---

*Try macadamia nuts for a different kind of crunch.

Lemon Nut Cookies

What could go better with our Lemon Nut Cookies than a tea party? If you like your tea straight up (unblended, unscented, and unherbed), look for loose teas that are usually more flavorful than the bagged variety.

¾ cup butter, softened
1½ cups sugar
2 eggs
1 tablespoon grated lemon rind
2 tablespoons lemon juice
2 teaspoons vanilla
2¾ cups flour
1 teaspoon baking soda
½ teaspoon cream of tartar
1 cup chopped pecans

1. Preheat oven to 400°F. Cream butter and sugar. Add eggs, lemon rind, lemon juice, and vanilla. Beat well. Add flour, baking soda, and cream of tartar. Beat until well mixed. Stir in pecans.

2. Using rounded teaspoonfuls, shape into 1-inch balls. Place 2 inches apart on ungreased cookie sheet.

3. Bake 8–10 minutes or until edges are lightly browned. Remove from cookie sheet immediately and cool on wire rack.

Makes 48 cookies

Aunt Marian's Mandel Bread

Everyone's got an aunt or a grandmother who makes a special kind of cookie for each holiday. In fact, you can count on her bringing them every time. So, in honor of Aunt Marian, try these solid, nutty cookies (they freeze well and you can even throw in a handful of mini-chocolate chips for variation).

BREAD
1 cup sugar
3 eggs
¾ cup corn oil
1 teaspoon vanilla
3 cups flour
3 teaspoons baking powder
½ cup walnuts
½ cup golden raisins (generous)

TOPPING
¼ cup sugar
½ tablespoon cinnamon

1. Preheat oven to 350°F. Grease a cookie sheet. In a large mixing bowl beat sugar and eggs together. Add oil and vanilla and mix well. Add flour and baking powder. Beat. Mix in walnuts and raisins. Mix cinnamon and sugar together and set aside.

2. Divide dough (it will be soft) into quarters. Pat each quarter out onto prepared cookie sheet into a rectangle 3 inches wide and between 5 and 6 inches long. Sprinkle each rectangle with 1 tablespoon of the cinnamon-sugar mixture.

3. Bake for 20 minutes. Remove from oven and cut each rectangle into 1-inch wide diagonal slices. Turn each slice on its side and return to oven for 10 more minutes. Remove from cookie sheet and cool on wire rack.

Makes 24 pieces

Peanut Butter Chocolate Bars

Thick and gooey, the peanut butter in these bars melts in your mouth, as well as on your hands! Without a doubt, these are two-handed bars—bite into one of these and be prepared to wipe quickly.

½ cup butter
1½ cups graham cracker crumbs
1 7-ounce package flaked coconut
1 14-ounce can sweetened condensed milk
½ cup chunky peanut butter
1 12-ounce package semisweet chocolate chips

1. Preheat oven to 350°F. Put butter in a 9″ × 13″ baking pan and set in oven to melt. Remove from oven and sprinkle evenly with graham cracker crumbs. Top with coconut and then pour milk over all.

2. Bake 25 minutes or until lightly browned. Remove from oven.

3. In small saucepan, over low heat, melt chocolate chips with peanut butter. Spread evenly over hot coconut layer. Cool 30 minutes and then refrigerate. Cut into bars.

Makes 36 bars

Mocha Pecan Cookies

Believe it or not, farmers in the state of New York sold $74,880,833.32 worth of eggs in 1986. Roughly translated, that's 400 trillion cookies!

1 cup semisweet chocolate chips
2 eggs
½ cup sugar
2 tablespoons flour
1 teaspoon baking powder
1 tablespoon instant coffee
   (not freeze-dried)
Pecan halves

1. Preheat oven to 375°F. Grease a cookie sheet. Melt chocolate chips in double boiler over hot water. Remove from hot water and set aside.

2. Beat eggs until thick. Gradually add sugar and continue beating until very thick. Mix flour, baking powder, and coffee together and blend into egg mixture. Add cooled chocolate and mix well.

3. Drop dough by scant teaspoonfuls, 1 inch apart, onto prepared cookie sheet. Carefully place 1 pecan half on center of each drop.

4. Bake 6–8 minutes or until lightly browned. Cool on wire rack.

Makes 70 cookies

Peanut Butter Chip Cookies

Peanut butter isn't just for kids anymore. A recent survey shows that adults eat half of all peanut butter consumed in the U.S., and are eating more each year. Don't spill the milk, save it for these cookies!

½ cup butter, softened
¾ cup brown sugar, firmly packed
½ cup chunky peanut butter
2 eggs
1½ cups flour
1 teaspoon baking soda
1 cup salted peanuts
1 6-ounce package semisweet chocolate
　　chips or butterscotch chips

1. Preheat oven to 350°F. Cream butter and brown sugar until light and fluffy. Add peanut butter and eggs and mix well. Stir in flour and baking soda and blend well. Add peanuts and chips. Mix just until blended.

2. Drop by rounded teaspoonfuls, 2 inches apart, onto ungreased cookie sheet.

3. Bake 9–12 minutes or until golden brown. Remove right away from cookie sheet and cool on wire rack.

Makes 48 cookies

Macadamia Nut Bars

Everyone seems to think macadamia nuts come to us exclusively from Hawaii when in fact they're grown around the world. We're not sure why this is the general perception, but nevertheless, the rumors abound and persist. If you're not a macadamia lover, why not substitute hazelnuts?

CRUST
1 cup flour
¼ cup sugar
½ cup butter

TOPPING
2 eggs
½ cup coconut
1½ cups brown sugar,
   firmly packed
1 cup macadamia nuts, chopped
2 tablespoons flour
1 teaspoon vanilla
½ teaspoon baking powder

1. Preheat oven to 350°F. Mix together flour and sugar. Cut in butter until crumbly. Pat into a 9″ square ungreased baking pan. Put in oven and bake 20 minutes.

2. Prepare topping. Beat eggs slightly. Add remainder of ingredients and mix until well blended. Pour over hot baked crust and return to oven for another 20 minutes.

3. Cool completely and cut into squares.

Makes 24 bars

Peanut Marshmallow Bars

These end up too gooey to ship, but they're easy and fun to make. Try freezing some for a cold sweet on a hot summer day.

½ cup sugar
½ cup brown sugar, firmly packed
½ cup butter, softened
½ cup creamy peanut butter
1 egg
½ teaspoon vanilla
1½ cups flour
2 teaspoons baking powder
½ teaspoon salt
1 7-ounce jar marshmallow creme
1 6-ounce package semisweet chocolate chips
¾ cup salted peanuts, chopped coarse

1. Preheat oven to 375°F. Cream sugars with butter and peanut butter. Add egg and vanilla and beat well. Stir in flour, baking powder, and salt. Mix well. Press into bottom and ¼ inch up the sides of an ungreased 10″ × 15″ jelly roll pan.

2. Spoon marshmallow creme over crust. Use wet knife to spread evenly to about ½ inch from side of pan. Sprinkle chocolate chips and peanuts over marshmallow creme.

3. Bake 12–15 minutes until light golden brown. Cool completely before cutting into bars.

Makes 36 bars

Peanutty Chips

Peter Piper picked a peck of pickled peppers, but forgot to pick up a pack of Peanutty Chips.

1½ cups flour, sifted
1 teaspoon salt
½ teaspoon baking soda
½ cup butter
½ cup chunky peanut butter
½ teaspoon cinnamon
1 cup sugar
2 eggs
½ cup water
1 cup semisweet chocolate chips
1 cup quick-cooking oats

1. Preheat oven to 375°F. Sift together already-sifted flour, salt, and baking soda. Set aside. Cream butter. Add peanut butter and cinnamon and beat. Gradually beat in sugar. Add eggs, one at a time, beating after each one. Add flour mixture, alternating with water. Beat well. Stir in chocolate chips and oats.

2. Drop by rounded teaspoonfuls, 2 inches apart, onto ungreased cookie sheet. Bake 12 minutes or until lightly browned. Cool on wire rack.

Makes 60 cookies

Pecan-Caramel Chocolate Bars

Three great tastes in one cookie bar. They're gooey, crunchy, and just melt away in your mouth. We don't recommend you tackle these cookies in the dead of summer, unless you live in Alaska.

CRUST
2 cups flour
1 cup brown sugar, firmly packed
½ cup unsalted butter, softened
1 cup pecan halves

FILLING
⅔ cup unsalted butter
½ cup brown sugar, firmly packed
½ cup butterscotch chips
½ cup semisweet chocolate chips

1. Preheat oven to 350°F. Combine flour, brown sugar, and butter. Beat with electric mixer at low speed, stopping to scrape sides of bowl, until crumbly. Press into ungreased 9″ × 13″ baking pan. Sprinkle with pecans. Set aside.

2. Prepare filling. In heavy pot, melt butter and brown sugar over medium heat. Stir constantly with wooden spoon until mixture boils all over (this will take 4–5 minutes). Continue stirring and boil for one minute. Pour carefully over crust with pecans.

3. Bake for 18–20 minutes or until filling is bubbly all over. Remove from oven and sprinkle with butterscotch and chocolate chips right away. Let sit for 5 minutes and then run a knife through chips zigzagging just enough to get a marbled effect.

4. Cool and cut into bars.

Makes 36 bars

Pecan Pie Bars

Pecans, that delightful nut best known to us in the shape of pies, originated here in North America. The Indians, long before the first Thanksgiving supper, used them as wonderful flavorings for all sorts of sweet treats. The settlers stood by their pies. In this recipe, we've combined the best of both worlds.

CRUST
2 cups flour
½ cup confectioners' sugar
1 cup butter

TOPPING
1 14-ounce can sweetened
  condensed milk
1 egg
1 teaspoon vanilla
1 16-ounce package almond
  brickle chips
1 cup chopped pecans

1. Preheat oven to 350°F. Combine flour and sugar; cut in butter until crumbly. Press firmly into bottom of a 9″ × 13″ ungreased baking pan. Bake 15 minutes.

2. Prepare topping. In a medium bowl, beat sweetened condensed milk, egg, and vanilla. Stir in chips and pecans. Spread evenly over baked crust. Return to oven and bake 25 minutes or until golden brown. Cool. Cut into bars. Store covered in refrigerator.

Makes 36 bars

Pecan Refrigerator Cookies

Have you ever wondered why no one has thought of selling cookies at the movies?

1 cup butter
¾ cup sugar
¾ cup dark brown sugar,
   firmly packed
2 teaspoons lemon juice
1 egg
1 egg yolk
3 cups flour
2 teaspoons baking powder
1 teaspoon cinnamon
1 cup chopped pecans
Confectioners' sugar

1. Cream butter and sugars until light and fluffy. Add lemon juice, egg, and egg yolk and mix well. Add flour, baking powder, cinnamon, and pecans and mix well.

2. Divide dough into thirds. Shape each third into a log 2 inches in diameter and wrap in wax paper. Refrigerate 6 hours or overnight.

3. Preheat oven to 400°F. Grease a cookie sheet. Remove logs one at a time and cut into ⅛-inch-thick slices. Place 1 inch apart on prepared cookie sheet. Bake for 7 minutes. Dust with confectioners' sugar while still warm. Cool on wire rack.

Makes 70 cookies

Poppy Seed Cookies

Poppy seeds, an ancient flavoring with eastern origins, has made its mark on Americana in the form of hot dog buns, egg bread, and bagels. This recipe incorporates the biting flavor of the poppy seed and a sweet butter base to create a surprisingly flavorful cookie.

1 cup butter
1½ cups confectioners' sugar
2 eggs
2 teaspoons vanilla
4 tablespoons poppy seeds
3 cups flour
½ cup ground walnuts

1. Cream butter and sugar. Add eggs and vanilla and beat until light and fluffy.

2. Combine poppy seeds, flour, and walnuts and add to butter mixture. Mix well.

3. Divide dough into thirds and form each third into a log, 1½ inches in diameter. Wrap each log in wax paper and refrigerate overnight.

4. Preheat oven to 375°F. Remove logs from refrigerator one at a time. Slice ⅛ inch thick (using very sharp knife), and place 2 inches apart onto ungreased cookie sheet. Bake for 10–15 minutes or until golden brown.

Makes 60 cookies

Sour Cream Cashew Cookies

We've discovered that people who eat cashews don't merely like them. Sometimes their affection for this premier nut goes beyond the bounds of even love—like cookies, people crave these nuts. Some even go to the extreme of picking out the cashews from a bowl of bridge mix. So, for your cashew-loving cookiemaniacs, try this recipe.

COOKIE
½ cup butter
1 cup dark brown sugar,
    firmly packed
1 egg
1 teaspoon vanilla
2 cups flour
¾ teaspoon baking soda
¾ teaspoon baking powder
½ cup sour cream
1½ cups roasted cashew
    nuts, chopped

FROSTING
¼ cup butter
2 tablespoons hot water
3 cups confectioners' sugar
2 tablespoons plus 2 teaspoons
    heavy cream

1. Preheat oven to 350°F. Grease a cookie sheet. Cream butter. Gradually add sugar. Add egg and vanilla; beat well. Add flour, baking soda, and baking powder, alternating with sour cream. Add nuts and blend well.

2. Drop by ½ teaspoonfuls, 1 inch apart, onto prepared cookie sheet and bake 10 minutes. Transfer to rack and frost while still warm.

3. Prepare frosting. Brown butter, remove from heat, and stir in water and confectioners' sugar. Add cream and mix well. Frost cookies.

Makes 60 cookies

Walnut Crescents ♥

This is another cookie from our original tin. We no longer make these wonderful cookies in their original crescent shape (though we encourage you to do so), as they are too fragile for shipping. Many of our customers think that this is the Mexican wedding cookie, or a Greek cookie. The only flavoring in this cookie is the vanilla, and we only use Nielsen/Massey vanilla, which we used to buy in 4-ounce bottles through a mail-order catalog. When we discovered that this extract was being made in virtually our own backyard, we prevailed upon Chet Nielsen to sell us a gallon. Currently we go through 50 gallons of vanilla each year.

1 cup butter
2 teaspoons vanilla
1½ cups ground walnuts
2⅔ cups sugar
2½ cups sifted flour
Confectioners' sugar

1. Preheat oven to 325°F. Cream butter. Add vanilla and then the nuts. Blend well. Add sugar. Mix. Add flour and beat with electric mixer on low until well blended. Dough will be stiff.

2. Pinch off a small piece of dough and roll into a 2-inch strip the diameter of a pencil. Place onto ungreased cookie sheet and gently bring ends down, forming a crescent.

3. Bake on upper rack 18–20 minutes or until just beginning to color.

4. Remove from cookie sheet and roll (very gently) in confectioners' sugar while still warm.

Makes 48 cookies

4
Sugar and Spice and Everything Nice

Brandy Snaps

Though extremely time consuming, Brandy Snaps aren't as difficult to make as your guests will give you credit for. We recommend you serve these cookies the same day you make them (they're worth the effort).

¼ **cup light corn syrup**
¼ **cup dark corn syrup**
½ **cup butter, softened**
1 **cup flour, sifted**
⅔ **cup sugar**
1 **teaspoon ground ginger**
1 **tablespoon brandy**

1. Preheat oven to 300°F. Grease a cookie sheet. Combine light and dark corn syrup in a medium saucepan over medium heat. Bring to a boil. Turn off heat and stir in butter until melted. Add flour, sugar, and ginger, stirring constantly; stir in brandy.

2. Drop dough by scant tablespoonfuls, 3 inches apart, onto prepared cookie sheet. Bake only four cookies at a time. Bake 8–10 minutes or until cookie is brown all over and stops bubbling. Remove from oven and loosen with spatula (carefully) using short strokes. Leave cookies on sheet for 45 seconds. Then, very quickly, roll each cookie around the handle of a wooden spoon to remove from sheet. Place on wire rack to cool.

Makes 40 cookies

Cinnamon Bars

We know some cookiemaniacs who are as passionate about hazelnuts as they are about cookies, so why not try substituting chopped hazelnuts for pecans in this recipe?

CRUST
2 cups flour
2 tablespoons cinnamon
⅛ teaspoon salt
1 cup butter, softened
½ cup light brown sugar,
    firmly packed
½ cup sugar
1 egg, separated
1½ cups pecans, chopped

TOPPING
½ cup sugar
1 tablespoon cinnamon

1. Preheat oven to 300°F. Combine flour, cinnamon, and salt and set aside. Cream butter, sugars, and egg yolk until light and fluffy. Add flour mixture and continue beating just until blended. Dough will be stiff.

2. Spread dough evenly in an ungreased 15½″ × 10½″ jelly roll pan. Beat egg white with fork, just until foamy. Spread evenly on top of batter. Sprinkle with nuts and press lightly into batter.

3. Bake for 35–40 minutes. Cut into bars while still hot. Let cool.

4. Mix cinnamon and sugar together and sprinkle on top of cooled (still a little warm) bars.

Makes 36 bars

Cinnamon Sugar Crisps

If you can find them, you might want to substitute black-walnut halves for the pistachio nuts. Black walnuts tend to have a more unusual earthy, nutty flavor, which is a nice change from the ordinary variety.

COOKIE
1 cup butter, softened
½ cup sugar
1 egg
2 teaspoons vanilla
2 cups flour
¼ teaspoon baking soda

TOPPING
½ cup sugar
1 teaspoon cinnamon
36 pistachio nuts (optional)

1. Preheat oven to 375°F. Grease a cookie sheet. Cream butter and sugar. Add egg and vanilla. Beat well. Add flour and baking soda. Beat until well mixed.

2. Prepare topping. In small bowl combine sugar and cinnamon.

3. Using rounded teaspoonfuls, shape dough into 1-inch balls. Roll in cinnamon-sugar mixture. Place 1 inch apart onto prepared cookie sheet. Press one pistachio nut into center of each cookie (optional).

4. Bake 10–14 minutes or until edges are lightly browned.

Makes 36 cookies

Ginger Cookies

These cookies are a nice way to end a Chinese meal, replacing the more ordinary almond cookie. Nothing, we're sure you'll agree, can replace the ubiquitous fortune cookie!

2 cups flour
1 teaspoon baking soda
¼ teaspoon salt
1 teaspoon ground ginger
¼ teaspoon ground cinnamon
¼ teaspoon ground cloves
½ cup butter
½ cup sugar
1 egg
½ cup molasses
Sugar (for rolling balls of dough in)

1. Sift together flour, baking soda, salt, ginger, cinnamon, and cloves. Set aside.

2. Cream together butter and ½ cup sugar until light and fluffy. Add egg and molasses and beat well. Gradually add flour mixture. Blend well.

3. Cover and refrigerate for 2 hours.

4. Preheat oven to 350°F. Grease a cookie sheet. Put sugar in shallow bowl. Remove dough from refrigerator.

5. Shape dough into 1-inch balls using two teaspoons. Roll balls in sugar and then place, about 2 inches apart, onto prepared cookie sheet.

6. Bake 12 minutes or until no imprint remains when cookies are lightly touched with finger. Remove from cookie sheet and cool on rack.

Makes 40 cookies

Molasses Cookies

Dark, thick, and rich, molasses is a flavoring that reminds us of the Old West. Technically, it is the dark brown syrup that is extracted from raw sugar during the refining process, but we prefer to think of it as the favored flavoring of the old wagon train cooks.

¾ **cup butter**
1 **cup sugar**
¼ **cup molasses (generous)**
1 **egg, lightly beaten**
1¾ **cups flour**
½ **teaspoon ground cloves**
½ **teaspoon ground ginger**
1 **teaspoon ground cinnamon**
½ **teaspoon salt**
½ **teaspoon baking soda**

1. Preheat oven to 350°F. Line a cookie sheet with aluminum foil. Melt butter in a saucepan. Add sugar and molasses and mix. Pour into mixing bowl and add lightly beaten egg. Sift flour with cloves, ginger, cinnamon, salt, and baking soda. Add to molasses mixture and mix well. Batter will be wet.

2. Drop by tablespoonfuls, 2 inches apart, onto foil-lined cookie sheet.

3. Bake 8–10 minutes or until cookies begin to darken, but are still soft. Remove from oven. Remove foil sheets and set aside to cool completely before removing cookies from foil.

Makes 24 cookies

Pumpkin Cookie Bars

As with pumpkin pie, it's very difficult to make these cookies from fresh pumpkin. Unfortunately. if you use canned pumpkin, you won't be able to roast the seeds.

CRUST
1 cup flour
½ cup quick-cooking oats
½ cup brown sugar,
    firmly packed
1¾ teaspoons cinnamon
½ cup butter, melted

FILLING
1 cup pumpkin puree
¾ cup evaporated milk
1 egg
⅓ cup sugar
½ teaspoon cinnamon
¼ teaspoon allspice
¼ teaspoon cloves, ground

FROSTING
1 8-ounce package cream
    cheese, softened
¼ cup orange marmalade

1. Preheat oven to 350°F. Combine flour, oats, brown sugar, and cinnamon. Add melted butter and mix well until crumbly. Press into bottom of an ungreased 9″ × 13″ baking pan and bake 20–25 minutes. Remove from oven and reduce temperature to 325°F.

2. Prepare filling. Combine pumpkin with evaporated milk, egg, sugar, cinnamon, allspice, and cloves. Beat well. Pour over crust. Bake at 325°F for 25–30 minutes or until toothpick inserted in center comes out clean. Cool completely.

3. Prepare frosting. Beat together cream cheese and orange marmalade until fluffy. Spread over cooled bars. Cut into bars.

Makes 32 bars

Soft Sugar Cookies

Honest! These cookies will just melt in your mouth, and won't leave anything on your hands. If you have a baby, this is a good cookie to make as your baby can safely gum it to crumbs.

3¼ cups flour
1 teaspoon baking soda
½ teaspoon salt
½ cup butter, softened
1 cup sugar
1 egg
1½ teaspoons vanilla
½ cup sour cream
70 raisins or nut halves (optional)

1. Preheat oven to 400°F. Grease a cookie sheet. Sift flour and then sift again with baking soda and salt. Cream butter. Add sugar, egg, and vanilla. Beat well. Add sour cream and one half of flour mixture. Beat, scraping bowl. Add balance of flour mixture and stir in by hand.

2. Divide dough in half and roll each half on a lightly floured surface to ¼-inch thickness. Sprinkle with sugar, roll in lightly. Cut with floured cutter, any size or shape.

3. Using a wide spatula lift cookies and set, 2 inches apart, onto prepared cookie sheet. If desired put a raisin or nut half in the center of each cookie.

4. Bake 8–10 minutes or until golden brown. Remove from cookie sheet and transfer to wire rack to cool.

Makes 70 cookies

Spice Spritz Cookies

For a small cookie, these really pack a punch. They're best served with plain tea, or even a glass of milk.

1 cup butter, softened
⅔ cup sugar
1 egg
1 teaspoon cinnamon
1 teaspoon nutmeg
½ teaspoon allspice
¼ teaspoon cloves, ground
2 teaspoons lemon juice
2 cups flour
Colored sugar (optional)

1. Preheat oven to 400°F. Grease a cookie sheet. Cream butter and sugar. Add egg and beat. Add spices and lemon juice and beat until light and fluffy. Stir in flour and mix by hand until well mixed, 3–4 minutes. Cover and refrigerate for 2 hours.

2. Remove dough from refrigerator and spoon into a cookie press. Using the design tip of your choice, form cookies, 1 inch apart, on prepared cookie sheet.

3. Bake 8–10 minutes or until edges are lightly browned. Sprinkle immediately with colored sugar, if desired.

4. Remove to wire rack to cool.

Makes 60 cookies

Sugar Crispies

The Butter Facts: in 1900, the average American consumed approximately 20 pounds of butter. Today, the average has fallen to less than 6 pounds per person per year, cookiemaniacs excluded.

1 cup butter
1 cup sugar
1 egg, separated
2 cups flour
1 teaspoon cinnamon
1 tablespoon water
Chopped walnuts

1. Cream butter and sugar. Add egg yolk, flour, and cinnamon. Beat well. Divide dough in half and shape into 2 logs. Wrap each log in wax paper and refrigerate at least 4 hours.

2. Preheat oven to 325°F. Remove 1 log at a time from refrigerator. Slice into ¼-inch-thick cookies and place, 1 inch apart, onto ungreased cookie sheet. Beat egg white with water. Brush on top of each cookie. Sprinkle with chopped walnuts. Bake 13 minutes. Remove from oven and transfer to wire rack to cool.

Makes 36 cookies

5
Butter, Cream Cheese, and Shortbread

Almond Butter Cookies

Did you know that a medium-size creamery produces an average of 3,600 pounds of butter per hour and that fully mechanized creameries make butter from sweet cream in five minutes?

1 cup butter
½ cup sugar
2 cups flour
½ cup ground almonds
Colored sugar

1. Preheat oven to 350°F. Cream butter and sugar until light and fluffy. Add flour and almonds and mix well.

2. Divide dough into fourths. Form each fourth into a log 1 inch in diameter. Put colored sugar on a long piece of wax paper and roll each log in sugar. Refrigerate until firm.

3. Cut into ½-inch slices and bake on ungreased cookie sheet 10 minutes. Remove from cookie sheet and cool on wire rack.

Makes 80 cookies

Butter Cookies ♥

Harrods, unarguably Britain's most famous department store, stocks dozens of butters in varying shades attesting to the individuality and seasonality of each county's creameries.

1 cup butter
⅔ cup sugar
2 egg yolks*
1 teaspoon vanilla or lemon extract
2⅔ cups flour

1. Preheat oven to 375°F. Cream butter; slowly add sugar, beating well. Beat in egg yolks, one at a time. Stir in vanilla or lemon extract and flour, beating slowly with a wooden spoon to make a smooth stiff dough.

2. Pinch off enough dough to make a ball 1 inch in diameter, rolling dough in the palms of your hands. Place 2 inches apart onto ungreased cookie sheet. Flatten each ball to desired thickness by pressing crosswise with lightly floured fork.

3. Bake for 10 minutes or until pale brown. Remove from cookie sheet while warm and cool on rack. At holiday times you could top with colored sprinkles.

Makes 24 cookies

---

*Left-over egg whites can be frozen, and you might want to use them for Meringue Kisses (see Index).

Cheesecake Bars

Cheesecake remains one of the most popular national desserts. Whole companies have been founded, factories set up, and people hired, for the sole purpose of producing cheesecake. New York boasts that it makes the best cheesecakes, but we think our recipe is far better.

CRUST
6 tablespoons butter,
  softened
⅓ cup brown sugar,
  firmly packed
1 cup flour
½ cup finely chopped walnuts

FILLING
¼ cup sugar
1 8-ounce package cream
  cheese, softened
2 tablespoons milk
1 tablespoon lemon juice
½ teaspoon vanilla
1 egg

1. Preheat oven to 350°F. Cream butter and brown sugar until light and fluffy. Add flour and walnuts and mix just until crumbly. Set aside ¾ cup for topping. Press remainder into bottom of an 8″ square ungreased baking pan. Bake for 12–15 minutes or until lightly browned. Remove from oven and set aside.

2. Prepare filling. In small bowl, blend sugar with cream cheese until smooth. Add milk, lemon juice, vanilla, and egg. Beat well. Spread over baked crust. Sprinkle with reserved crumb mixture.

3. Return to oven and bake 25 minutes. Remove from oven. Cool, cut into bars. Refrigerate.

Makes 20 bars

Chocolate Chip Shortbread

The Walker clan made shortbread famous worldwide, sparking curiosity as to the origin of the name. Rumor has it that shortbread, way back in the Middle Ages, was originally baked in pie pans, then topped with filling and cream. Wethinks no one really knows how this terrific cookie got its name.

2 cups butter, softened
2 cups confectioners' sugar
2 teaspoons vanilla
$\frac{1}{2}$ teaspoon salt
$4\frac{1}{2}$ cups flour
1 12-ounce package
    semisweet chocolate chips
Confectioners' sugar
    (for sprinkling on cookies)

1. Preheat oven to 350°F. Cream butter and confectioners' sugar. Blend in vanilla and salt. Gradually stir in flour until well blended. Mix in chocolate chips. Dough will be stiff.

2. Pinch off about an inch of dough and roll into a ball, using palms of hands. Place 2 inches apart onto ungreased cookie sheet. Flatten with a fork to $1\frac{1}{2}$-inch rounds.

3. Bake 15 minutes or until light golden. Remove from tray while warm and place on wire rack. Sprinkle lightly with confectioners' sugar.

Makes 90 cookies

Cream Cheese Bars

These are a house favorite, but one we don't include in our tin due to its perishability (in other words, don't try to ship this one). We created these one day while standing in Jeri's kitchen, trying to make a cheesecake. We ended up adding leftover orange rind from another recipe and whatever else was in the kitchen (no sink, though).

CRUST
2 cups graham cracker crumbs
⅔ cup butter, melted
¼ cup sugar

FILLING AND TOPPING
1 8-ounce package cream
   cheese, softened
½ cup sugar
1 teaspoon grated orange rind
1 egg
1 6-ounce package semisweet
   chocolate chips
¾ cup flaked coconut
½ cup chopped walnuts

1. Preheat oven to 350°F. In small bowl, combine graham cracker crumbs, melted butter, and sugar. Mix well with a fork. Press into bottom of ungreased 9″ × 13″ baking pan. Bake for 8 minutes. Remove from oven and set aside.

2. Prepare filling and topping. Combine cream cheese, sugar, orange rind, and egg. Beat well until smooth. Pour over baked crust. Sprinkle evenly with chocolate chips, coconut, and walnuts.

3. Return to oven and bake 25–30 minutes or until coconut turns golden brown. Cool completely. Cut into bars.

Makes 36 bars

Cream Cheese Butter Cookies ♥

This is one of our original bestselling cookies and it remains the only cookie we can't resist as it comes right out of the oven (it always results in a few burned fingers!). This is our signature logo cookie, and we make it two ways: heart-shaped for our tin and round, large, and sprinkled with sugar. It's an all-time favorite.

> **2½ cups flour, sifted**
> **½ teaspoon salt**
> **¼ teaspoon cinnamon**
> **1 cup butter**
> **3 ounces cream cheese**
> **1 cup sugar**
> **1 egg yolk**
> **1 teaspoon vanilla**
> **1 teaspoon grated orange rind**

1. Preheat oven to 350°F. Sift together already-sifted flour with salt and cinnamon and set aside. Cream butter and cream cheese together. Gradually add sugar and mix well. Beat in egg yolk, vanilla, and orange rind. Slowly blend in flour, salt, and cinnamon mixture.

2. Dough will not need to be refrigerated unless your kitchen is very warm. If using a cookie cutter, dough should be rolled out on a floured board ¼ inch thick. Use any size or shape cookie cutter, or any disc shape for cookie press. We have used a heart-shaped cutter.

3. Using any type of cookie cutter or cookie press, form cookies on ungreased cookie sheet 1 inch apart. Bake 12–15 minutes. Remove from oven and transfer to wire rack to cool.

Makes 48 cookies

Lemon Butter Cookies

Cookie: Small flat or slightly raised baked cake.
Mania: Unswerving enthusiasm.

½ cup unsalted butter, softened
½ cup sugar
1 egg yolk
¼ cup fresh lemon juice
1½ teaspoons grated lemon rind
Pinch of salt
1 cup less 2 tablespoons flour, sifted
Confectioners' sugar

1. Preheat oven to 375°F. Grease a cookie sheet. Cream butter and sugar until light and fluffy. Mix in yolk, then lemon juice, lemon rind, and salt. Fold in flour.

2. Drop by teaspoonfuls, about 2 inches apart, onto prepared sheet.

3. Bake 10 minutes or until edges of cookies begin to brown. Leave on baking sheets to cool slightly and then transfer to wire rack. Dust with confectioners' sugar and cool completely.

Makes 36 cookies

Lemon-Glazed Butter Cookies

We recommend you make the lemon glaze as tart as possible, so it will contrast nicely with the rich butter-cookie base. Also, you might try adding a piece of lemon peel on top before the glaze sets.

COOKIE
1 cup unsalted butter, softened
⅓ cup confectioners' sugar
1 cup flour
⅔ cup cornstarch

GLAZE
2½ cups confectioners' sugar, sifted
½ cup butter, melted
2 tablespoons fresh lemon juice

1. Preheat oven to 350°F. Beat together butter and ⅓ cup confectioners' sugar with electric mixer on medium speed for 1 minute. Sift together flour and cornstarch. Add to butter and sugar mixture. Blend until dough is soft, about 1 minute. Drop by teaspoonfuls, 2 inches apart, onto ungreased cookie sheet. Bake 15 minutes or until very lightly browned. Remove from cookie sheet and cool on wire rack.

2. Prepare glaze. Combine 2½ cups confectioners' sugar, melted butter, and lemon juice. While cookies are still warm, mound ½ teaspoon icing on each. Icing will melt. Cool cookies.

Makes 36 cookies

Ribbon Butter Cookies

Twelve states account for 95 percent of all butter produced in the United States. And guess who leads the stick? Yup, Wisconsin—the Dairy State.

2 cups unsalted butter, softened
2 cups sugar
2 eggs
1 tablespoon vanilla
½ teaspoon salt
5 cups flour, sifted

1. Preheat oven to 375°F. Cream butter and sugar until light in color. Mix in eggs, vanilla, and salt. Stir in flour with wooden spoon. Transfer dough to cookie press with ribbon attachment. Press dough onto ungreased cookie sheet in 6-to-10-inch-long strips*.

2. Bake 8–10 minutes or until golden brown. Remove from cookie sheet and cool on wire rack.

Makes 40 cookies

---

*Chocolate shots, colored sprinkles, or other optional decorations may be added at this time.

Shortbread Cookies

For all the right reasons (its creamy taste and crumbly texture), shortbread remains one of the most frequently exported products in Great Britain. It is said that Queen Elizabeth, when in residence at her Scottish home Balmoral, likes to take shortbread with her tea.

2 cups unsalted butter
1 cup confectioners' sugar
3 cups sifted flour
1 cup rice flour (can substitute
   all-purpose sifted flour)

1. Cream butter. Add confectioners' sugar gradually. Blend well, do not overbeat. Gradually work in all the flour.

2. Turn dough out onto a lightly floured board and pat out.

3. Divide into 2 circles. Put on cookie sheet and pat out to ¾ inch thick. Pinch edges and prick all over with a fork. Refrigerate dough on sheet for ½ hour. Preheat oven to 375°F.

4. Remove cookie sheet from refrigerator. Bake for 5 minutes, then lower heat to 300°F and bake for 45–60 minutes, until golden.

5. Remove from oven and cut into wedges while still warm.

Makes 32 wedges

Spicy Butter Thins

This cookie is a terrific companion to the Spice Spritz cookie recipe (see Index). Both are elegant, and yet add that zing to a dessert tray. You might try serving this cookie with a plain ice cream or sorbet.

¾ cup flour
¼ cup sugar
1 teaspoon cinnamon
1 teaspoon instant coffee
   (not crystals)
½ teaspoon ginger
⅔ cup butterscotch chips
½ cup butter
1 egg
½ cup salted peanuts, chopped
⅓ cup butterscotch chips

1. Preheat oven to 300°F. Combine flour, sugar, cinnamon, instant coffee, and ginger. Set aside.

2. Melt ⅔ cup butterscotch chips in top of double boiler over hot water. Add butter. Melt together and mix. Remove from heat. Blend in egg and flour mixture. Mix well. Spread on 10″ × 15″ ungreased jelly roll pan. Sprinkle with peanuts and ⅓ cup butterscotch chips.

3. Bake 25–30 minutes or until lightly browned. Remove from oven and cut into bars. Remove from pan immediately. Cool.

Makes 36 bars

Sour Cream Wreaths

This is one of our most popular Christmas cookies. Though we do say to use red or green colored sugar, any color (depending on the holiday or festival) would be fine to use. You might try alternating colors for a particularly festive plate.

1 cup butter
1 cup sugar
½ cup sour cream
¼ teaspoon salt
1 teaspoon vanilla
3 cups flour
Colored sugar (red or green)

1. Cream butter in large mixing bowl. Slowly add sugar. Beat well. Add sour cream, salt, and vanilla, mixing well. Gradually add flour and blend well.

2. Divide dough in half and wrap each half separately in wax paper. Refrigerate at least two hours.

3. Preheat oven to 400°F. Grease a cookie sheet. Put colored sugar in small, shallow bowl. Remove one package of dough at a time from refrigerator. Roll dough into a long rope the width of a pencil and cut into 4-inch pieces. Overlap ends slightly to form wreath. Pat each one into bowl of colored sugar and turn over onto prepared cookie sheet (sugared side up) 1 inch apart.

4. Bake 10–12 minutes. Remove while warm from cookie sheets and cool on wire racks.

Makes 75 cookies

6
More than Just Oatmeal

Caramel Bars

We bet you never thought oatmeal could taste so good (but Mr. Quaker Oats would have disagreed). These bars are an attractive way to get the most out of your caramels.

1 cup plus 2 tablespoons flour
¼ teaspoon salt
¼ teaspoon baking soda
½ cup brown sugar, firmly packed
¾ cup quick-cooking oats
½ cup butter
24 light-colored caramel candies
2 tablespoons cream
½ cup semisweet chocolate chips

1. Preheat oven to 350°F. Grease an 8″ square baking pan. Combine 1 cup flour, salt, baking soda, brown sugar, and oats. Cut in butter until dough is the texture of cornmeal. Remove 1 cup and set aside. Press remaining mixture into bottom of prepared pan. Bake 10 minutes. Remove from oven and set aside.

2. Combine caramels and cream in top of double boiler. Cook over boiling water until caramels melt. Blend in 2 tablespoons flour. Spread evenly over baked crust. Sprinkle with chocolate chips and then put the reserved crumb mixture on top.

3. Return to oven and bake 12–15 minutes or until lightly browned. Cut into bars while still slightly warm.

Makes 24 bars

Mince Oatmeal Cookies

Mincemeat is, perhaps, best known in pies. In England, miniature mince pies are a wonderful treat you share with your neighbors. Usually someone makes about a hundred and then parcels them out in baskets or hampers at Christmas. Our cookie captures the taste of those pies, but puts it into a cookiemaniac's favorite shape.

3 cups quick-cooking oats
1½ cups light brown sugar,
   firmly packed
1½ cups flour
1 teaspoon baking soda
½ teaspoon salt
½ cup vegetable oil
3 eggs, beaten
3 tablespoons water
1 9-ounce package condensed
   mincemeat, crumbled

1. Preheat oven to 350°F. Grease a cookie sheet.

2. Stir together oats, brown sugar, flour, baking soda, and salt in large bowl. Add oil, eggs, and water; mix well. Stir in mincemeat.

3. Drop by rounded teaspoonfuls, 2 inches apart, onto prepared cookie sheet. Bake 8–10 minutes or until lightly browned. Remove immediately to wire racks for cooling.

Makes 60 cookies

Oatmeal-Apricot Bars

Oatmeal-Apricot Bars are a pretty addition to your party plate, as well as being one of the quickest and easiest recipes in this book. For variation, you might try substituting other flavors of preserves, such as blackberry, raspberry, or strawberry.

CRUST
1¼ cups flour
1¼ cups quick-cooking oats
½ cup sugar
¾ cup butter, melted
½ teaspoon baking soda
2 teaspoons vanilla

FILLING
1 12-ounce jar apricot preserves
½ cup flaked coconut

1. Preheat oven to 350°F. Grease a 9″ × 13″ baking pan. Combine flour, oats, and sugar in mixing bowl. Add melted butter, baking soda, and vanilla. Beat with electric mixer at low speed, stopping often to scrape sides of bowl, until crumbly. Remove 1 cup and set aside; press remaining mixture into prepared pan.

2. Spread apricot preserves on top of crust keeping ½ inch away from edge. Add coconut to reserved crumb mixture and sprinkle on top of preserves.

3. Bake 25 minutes or until edges are lightly browned. Cool and cut into bars.

Makes 36 bars

Oatmeal-Butterscotch Drops

This is a delightful concoction we like to serve with our Peanut Butter Chocolate Bars. Butterscotch, with its unique flavor, is made from brown sugar, corn syrup, butter, and water, and not from scotch and butter, as is commonly thought by adults under the age of 21.

  1 cup flour
  1½ cups sugar
  ½ teaspoon salt
  ¾ cup milk
  ¼ cup butter
  1 6-ounce package
    butterscotch morsels
  2½ cups quick-cooking oats
  1 cup flaked coconut
  1 cup chopped walnuts
  1 teaspoon vanilla

1. Preheat oven to 325°F. Lightly grease a cookie sheet. Combine flour, sugar, salt, milk, and butter in a 3-quart saucepan. Bring to a boil over low heat, stirring occasionally. Boil 3 minutes, stirring constantly. Remove from heat. Stir in butterscotch morsels. Add oats, coconut, walnuts, and vanilla. Mix well.

2. Drop by tablespoonfuls, 2 inches apart, onto prepared cookie sheet. Bake 12–15 minutes. Cool 2 minutes on cookie sheet and then remove to wire rack.

Makes 36 cookies

Oatmeal-Chocolate Bars

Talk about hearty, these bars are enough to satisfy even a cookiemaniac's passion for the great taste of oats and chocolate. (As we all know, a cookiemaniac's cravings are like a bear foraging for his breakfast after a winter's hibernation.)

FILLING
2 tablespoons butter
1 6-ounce package semisweet
    chocolate chips
1 5⅓-ounce can
    evaporated milk
¼ cup sugar
½ teaspoon vanilla

CRUST
½ cup butter, softened
1 cup brown sugar,
    firmly packed
1 egg
1 teaspoon vanilla
1¼ cups flour
½ teaspoon baking soda
2 cups quick-cooking oats
1 cup walnuts, chopped

1. Preheat oven to 350°F. Grease a 9″ square baking pan. Prepare filling: In medium saucepan, combine all ingredients. Over medium heat bring to a rolling boil, stirring constantly. Remove from heat and cool.

2. Prepare crust. Cream butter. Add sugar and beat. Add egg and vanilla and beat until light and fluffy. Stir in flour, baking soda, oats, and walnuts. Blend well.

3. Spread half of mixture into bottom of prepared pan. Spread with cooled chocolate mixture. Crumble balance of oatmeal mixture on top.

4. Bake 25–30 minutes or until golden brown. Cool completely before cutting into squares.

Makes 36 bars

Oatmeal-Raisin-Chip Cookies

There is a never-ending battle between cookiemaniacs who love chocolate chip cookies and those who love oatmeal raisin cookies. We created our Oatmeal-Raisin-Chip cookie to strike a compromise for the sake of cookie lovers everywhere. Enjoy!

2 cups flour
1 teaspoon baking soda
1 teaspoon cinnamon
¼ teaspoon salt
1 cup butter
1 cup sugar
1 cup light brown sugar,
**   firmly packed**
2 eggs
1 teaspoon vanilla
2 cups quick-cooking oatmeal
1 6-ounce package semisweet
**   chocolate chips**
1 cup dark seedless raisins
¾ cup pecans, chopped

1. Preheat oven to 375°F. Grease a cookie sheet. Combine flour, baking soda, cinnamon, and salt and set aside.

2. Cream butter. Add sugars and beat. Add eggs and vanilla and beat until light and fluffy. Stir in flour mixture a little at a time, scraping bowl and beating after each addition. Add oatmeal and beat well. Stir in chocolate chips, raisins, and pecans.

3. Drop by tablespoonfuls, 2 inches apart, onto prepared cookie sheet. Bake 9–12 minutes or until golden brown. Cool on wire rack.

Makes 90 cookies

Oatmeal Surprise Bars

We'll tell you ahead of time: the surprise is the caramel filling inside. Fans of this bar tell us it reminds them of a sundae. That's silly, we tell them, who ever heard of an oatmeal sundae?

½ cup butter
1½ cups quick-cooking
    oatmeal
¾ cup flour
½ cup brown sugar,
    firmly packed
½ teaspoon baking soda
¼ teaspoon salt
1 6-ounce package semisweet
    chocolate chips
½ cup walnuts, chopped
⅓ cup caramel-flavored
    ice cream topping
5 teaspoons flour

1. Preheat oven to 350°F. Grease a 9″ square baking pan. In medium saucepan melt butter over low heat. Remove from heat. Add oatmeal, flour, sugar, baking soda, and salt and mix well. Press half of the mixture into the bottom of the prepared pan. Set aside balance of mixture. Bake 10 minutes.

2. Remove from oven and sprinkle with chocolate chips and nuts. Combine caramel topping with 5 teaspoons flour and drizzle over nuts. Sprinkle remaining oatmeal mixture over top.

3. Return to oven and bake 15–20 minutes or until golden brown. Cool. Refrigerate to make cutting easier.

Makes 24 bars

7
Specialties of the House

Butterscotch Refrigerator Cookies

What's nice about our refrigerator cookies is that once you've rolled them into a log (using a sheet of wax paper), they're easy to pop into the refrigerator for storing, and then pop out for as many hot, fresh cookies as you can eat.

2¾ cups sifted flour
2 teaspoons baking powder
½ teaspoon salt
½ cup butter
2 cups brown sugar,
   firmly packed
2 eggs
1 teaspoon vanilla
½ cup chopped walnuts

1. Sift flour. Add baking powder and salt and sift again. Set aside.

2. Cream butter. Add brown sugar, eggs, and vanilla. Beat until light and fluffy. Add flour mixture and mix well. Add nuts and stir.

3. Form dough into 2 logs, each about 2½ inches in diameter. Wrap in wax paper and refrigerate at least 4 hours.

4. Preheat oven to 400°F. Remove logs from refrigerator one at a time. Slice cookies ¼ inch thick and place ½ inch apart onto ungreased cookie sheet. Bake 8–10 minutes or until light brown around the edges. Remove from cookie sheet and cool on wire racks.

Makes 48 cookies

Florentines

Daniel Peter (a Swiss chocolate maker) perfected the process of making milk (sweet) chocolate in 1876. By definition, chocolate liqueur (nonalcoholic) must constitute 10 percent of a milk-chocolate product. In this fancy party cookie recipe, the milk chocolate and candied orange rind complement each other elegantly.

¾ cup whipping cream
¼ cup sugar
¼ cup flour
½ cup finely chopped almonds
2 2-ounce jars (4 ounces total)
   candied orange peel, finely chopped
8 ounces sweet cooking chocolate

1. Preheat oven to 350°F. Grease and flour a cookie sheet. Pour cream into a medium-size bowl. Stir in sugar by hand until dissolved. Add flour, almonds, and orange peel and mix by hand until well blended. Do not use electric mixer.

2. Drop batter by level teaspoonfuls, 4 inches apart, onto prepared cookie sheet. Use back of spoon to spread each into a 2-inch round.

3. Bake 10–12 minutes or until lightly browned. Let cool 1 minute and then remove with spatula to wire rack. Regrease and reflour sheet between baking.

4. Melt chocolate in top of double boiler over hot water or in microwave. Spread on bottom of each cookie and put on wax paper–lined cookie sheet. Refrigerate until chocolate is firm.

Makes 36 cookies

The Dip and Sprinkle ♥

We know The Dip and Sprinkle sounds like a hip dance from the 1960s, but please believe us that it's been a house specialty from the word go. It's a favorite Christmas cookie treat as it is festively decorated with brightly colored sprinkles. We would dip and sprinkle for weeks on end just to fill our Christmas orders. Although we originally sold this cookie in our tin, we no longer include these in our regular assortment.

COOKIE
2⅓ cups sifted flour
¼ teaspoon salt
1 cup butter, softened
⅔ cup sugar
1 egg yolk
1 teaspoon vanilla
1 cup finely ground
    unblanched almonds

CHOCOLATE DIPPING MIXTURE
1 6-ounce package semisweet
    chocolate chips
3 tablespoons butter
1 tablespoon hot water
Chocolate shots or multicolored
    sprinkles (optional)

1. Sift already-sifted flour with salt and set aside. In large bowl, cream butter with electric mixer at medium speed. Add sugar, egg yolk, and vanilla. Beat until light and fluffy. Gradually add flour and salt mixture and almonds, mixing until well blended.

2. Shape dough into two logs, each 1½ inches in diameter, and wrap in wax paper. Refrigerate until firm, at least 2 hours.

3. Preheat oven to 350°F. Lightly grease a cookie sheet. Using a ruler, mark each log at ¼-inch intervals. With a sharp, thin knife cut into slices and put onto prepared cookie sheet 1 inch apart.

4. Bake 8–10 minutes or until lightly browned. Remove from cookie sheet and cool on rack.

5. Prepare chocolate mixture. In top of double boiler over hot water, melt chocolate chips and butter. Stir in hot water.

6. Lay sheet of wax paper on table. Dip half of cookie into hot chocolate mixture and put on wax paper.

7. If using sprinkles dip a few cookies and then sprinkle with chocolate shots or multicolored sprinkles while chocolate is still wet. Leave on wax paper at least an hour to dry.

Makes 60 cookies

Kisses

We truly believe that by making our Kisses cookie, you show your cookiemaniac just how much you love him or her. We make these cookies for our very favorite friends, and they always delight even the most finicky appetites.

1 cup butter
½ cup sugar
1 teaspoon vanilla
2 cups flour
1 14-ounce bag Hershey chocolate kisses
Confectioners' sugar

1. Cream butter and sugar, beating well. Add vanilla and flour and mix well. Chill dough for 1 hour.

2. Preheat oven to 375°F. Pinch off a piece of dough. Roll into ball with palms of hands and then flatten. Dough should not be thick. Put kiss in center. Bring dough up, shaping around kiss to cover completely.

3. Place onto ungreased cookie sheet 1 inch apart and bake for 12–15 minutes, until just starting to brown.

4. Roll in confectioners' sugar when cool.

Makes 60 cookies

Lace Cookies

Lace cookies are easy-to-make, beautiful sandwich cookies that are sure to impress your guests. Lace cookies are named for the lacelike quality of the baked cookie. The chocolate will effectively "glue" two cookies together, and the sandwich freezes exceptionally well in an airtight container.

½ cup butter
1 cup quick-cooking oats
  (not instant)
½ cup light brown sugar
⅓ cup flour
2 tablespoons milk
¼ teaspoon salt
4 ounces semisweet chocolate

1. Preheat oven to 350°F. Grease a large cookie sheet. In medium saucepan melt butter. Remove from heat. Stir in remaining ingredients except chocolate.

2. Drop batter by level teaspoonfuls, 2 inches apart, onto prepared cookie sheet. Make only six on one sheet.

3. Bake 7–9 minutes or until lightly browned. Let stand for 1 minute, then remove with large spatula to table covered with aluminum foil or baking paper to cool. Do not cool on a rack! When all cookies are baked and cooled, melt chocolate in top of double boiler. With a small knife or spatula, spread the bottom of one cookie with chocolate and sandwich it with the bottom of another cookie. Repeat with remaining cookies and chocolate. Store in airtight container in refrigerator or freezer.

Makes 24 cookies

Meringue Kisses

The nice thing about making Meringue Kisses at the same time you make our Butter cookies is that you'll use three whole eggs (separated) for both recipes, and you won't have to worry about storing the leftovers. These are lovely holiday cookies, as you can decorate the Kisses with colored sprinkles or silver chocolate shots.

3 egg whites
1 teaspoon vanilla
¼ teaspoon cream of tartar
Dash of salt
1 cup superfine sugar
1 6-ounce package semisweet
    chocolate chips and/or
    6 ounces chopped pecans

1. Preheat oven to 250°F. In small mixing bowl, combine egg whites, vanilla, cream of tartar, and salt. Beat to soft peaks. Very gradually add sugar, beating until very stiff peaks form. Meringue will be glossy. Drop in chocolate chips and/or chopped pecans and mix gently.

2. Drop by teaspoonfuls, about 1½ inches apart, onto ungreased cookie sheet or cookie sheet lined with aluminum foil. (At Christmas time sprinkle meringues with red or green sugar crystals.)

3. Bake for 45 minutes. Remove from baking sheet while warm, and cool.

Makes 24 cookies

Potato Chip Cookies

If you can't seem to get enough of the salty goodness of potato chips (and we're not differentiating between ruffles and ridges), then this recipe is for you. Believe us, when we first heard about this recipe we couldn't imagine how it would taste. But when we tried it we found it to be wonderfully buttery with delicious crunchy bits.

2 cups butter, softened
1 cup sugar
3½ cups flour, sifted
2 teaspoons vanilla
2 cups crushed potato chips

1. Preheat oven to 350°F. Cream butter and sugar until light and fluffy. Add flour and vanilla and mix well. Stir in potato chips.

2. Drop by rounded teaspoonfuls, 1 inch apart, onto ungreased cookie sheet. Flatten with a fork.

3. Bake 12 minutes. Remove from oven and place on wire rack to cool.

Makes 42 cookies

Sesame Wafers

The sesame seed comes from an ancient East Indian annual herb, the seeds and oil of which are used today as flavorings. As legend has it, sesame is also a secret password Aladdin used to gain entry to his mother's ever-locked cookie jar.

2 cups flour, sifted
½ teaspoon baking soda
½ teaspoon salt
1 cup butter
1 cup sugar
1 egg
1 teaspoon vanilla
4 ounces sesame seeds (about ½ cup)

1. Sift together already-sifted flour, soda, and salt. Set aside. Cream butter with sugar until light and fluffy. Beat in egg and vanilla. Blend in flour, half at a time, mixing well. Dough will be soft. Divide in half and wrap in wax paper. Refrigerate at least 3 hours.

2. Preheat oven to 350°F. Lightly grease a cookie sheet. Put sesame seeds in small bowl. By teaspoonfuls, roll dough in palms of hands, then roll in sesame seeds.

3. Place 2 inches apart onto prepared cookie sheet. Bake 8–10 minutes until light golden. Remove from cookie sheet and cool on wire rack.

Makes 96 wafers

Alfie and Archie's Dog Biscuits

For your dogs only. This recipe, the 101st in Cookiemania *(but who's counting?), was created, spur of the moment, during party preparations. The smell of the main course (a juicy roast) had our dogs jumping up and down in anticipation. To quiet them down, we created these dog biscuits. Alfie and Archie love them—we hope your dog will, too.*

2½ cups whole wheat flour
½ cup powdered dry milk
½ teaspoon salt
½ teaspoon garlic powder
1 teaspoon brown sugar
6 tablespoons meat drippings
   (fat from any beef or lamb
   you have cooked)
1 egg, beaten
½ cup ice water

1. Preheat oven to 350°F. Lightly oil a cookie sheet. Combine flour, dry milk, salt, garlic powder, and sugar. Cut in meat drippings until mixture resembles cornmeal. Mix in egg. Add enough water so that mixture forms a ball.

2. Using your fingers, pat out dough onto cookie sheet to ½ inch thick. Cut with a cookie cutter (you can buy one in the shape of a bone) or a knife (cut a bone shape) and remove scraps. (Scraps can be formed again and baked.)

3. Bake 25–30 minutes. Remove from tray and cool on rack.

Makes about 10 dog biscuits (from a 6-inch cutter)

Index